The
OPEN

The
OPEN
A Twentieth-century History

FRANCIS MURRAY

PAVILION

THIS BOOK IS DEDICATED TO MY MOTHER DOROTHY, MY
THREE CHILDREN LUCY, ANGUS AND FREDDIE AND TO ALL
FOLLOWERS OF LINKS GOLF, TO MY MIND THE FINEST
FORM OF THIS GREAT GAME.

First published in Great Britain in 2000 by
PAVILION BOOKS LIMITED
London House, Great Eastern Wharf
Parkgate Road, London SW11 4NQ

Designed by David Fordham.

A CIP catalogue record for this book is available
from the British Library.

ISBN 1 86205 465 7

Set in Galliard and Nicolas Cochin by MATS, Southend-on-Sea
Colour origination by Anglia
Printed and bound in Italy by Conti Tipocolor

10 9 8 7 6 5 4 3 2 1

This book can be ordered direct from the publisher.
Please contact the Marketing Department but try your
bookshop first.

CONTENTS

FOREWORD BY GARY PLAYER   7

THE MEN BEHIND THE SCENES   8

INTRODUCTION   9

THE EARLY YEARS **1860–1900**   11

THE GREAT TRIUMVIRATE – VARDON, BRAID, TAYLOR **1900–1914**   17

THE GOLDEN YEARS **1920–1933**   35

COTTON LEADS THE BRITISH COMEBACK **1934–1939**   57

THE ERA OF LOCKE AND THOMSON **1946–1959**   67

ARNOLD PALMER REVITALIZES THE CHAMPIONSHIP **1960–1962**   91

THE ERA OF NICKLAUS, PLAYER AND TREVINO **1963–1974**   97

THE WATSON YEARS **1975–1983**   125

THE ERA OF BALLESTEROS, NORMAN AND FALDO **1984–1993**   147

A NEW GENERATION TAKES OVER **1994–2000**   171

MILESTONES: 140 YEARS OF THE OPEN CHAMPIONSHIP   188

OPEN RECORDS   191

THE OPEN COURSES   192

OPEN RESULTS   214

FACTS AND FIGURES   219

BIBLIOGRAPHY   221

ACKNOWLEDGEMENTS   222

INDEX   223

THE EARLY YEARS
1860–1900

Until his untimely death from jaundice in 1859 Allan Robertson, a club-and ball-maker born and based in St Andrews, was considered the finest golfer of his time. It is believed that the Open Championship arose out of a desire to determine his successor. With the support and enthusiasm of the 13th Earl of Eglinton, a keen and influential figure in Scottish sport, and Major (later Colonel) James Fairlie, the first Open Championship was held at Prestwick, on the Ayrshire coast of Scotland on 17 October 1860.

Each club in Scotland was invited to send its professional, and just eight entrants played over three rounds of the 12-hole course.

There was no prize money, but a Championship Belt was commissioned. Similar to a champion prize-fighter's belt, it was made from red Moroccan leather with silver panels. The Belt was to be presented to the winner each year and awarded outright to anyone who won the event in three successive years. Willie Park, of the Musselburgh club near Edinburgh, was the first winner with a score of 174, two strokes less than Tom Morris, at that time the professional at the home club of Prestwick.

Strictly speaking the first true 'Open' was held the following year when the leading amateurs were also invited to compete. They have been ever since, but to date only three amateurs have won the championship: John Ball, Harold Hilton (twice) and Bobby Jones (three times).

The first eight championships, never with more than 17 competitors, were all held at Prestwick and were dominated by Tom Morris and Willie Park, Morris winning four and Park three.

LEFT: *Allan Robertson whose death is thought to have led to the creation of the Open Championship.*

RIGHT: *Allan Robertson lining up a putt at St Andrews circa 1856. Watching him closely from left to right are: James Wilson, William Dow, Willie Dunn, Willie Park Sr, Old Tom Morris, Daw Anderson and Bob Kirk.*

RIGHT: *The most famous golfing family of the 19th Century if not of all time. Old Tom Morris and his son Young Tom won four Open titles each. Young Tom was acknowledged as the better player but he tragically died aged just 24 years. His father lived to the ripe old age of 87 before dying in St Andrews in 1908.*

RIGHT: *A picture to celebrate the Open Championship's jubilee in 1910 showing the Great Triumvirate surrounded by all the champions going back to the event's beginnings in 1860.*

In 1863 the professionals shared a purse of £10, but it was not until the following year that a financial first prize was given. For his victory Tom Morris's reward was £6.

In the years 1868–70 the championship was won by Tom Morris's son, also called Tom, and from now on we shall refer to Morris Senior and Junior as Old Tom and Young Tom respectively! Young Tom was to dominate the championship for several years, consistently recording lower scores year by year. His three-round score of 149 in 1870 was some 25 strokes less than that recorded by his father in the inaugural Open in 1860.

Young Tom remains the youngest winner of the Open Championship, or any of the other Majors – at 17 years and 161 days – and he also had the distinction of achieving the first hole in one in the Open, on the 8th at Prestwick in 1868.

Having won the Open in three successive years, Young Tom was therefore awarded the Belt outright. Originally his family kept it, but it can be seen today in the clubhouse of the Royal & Ancient Golf Club at St Andrews.

No championship was held in 1871, as the authorities had not organized an alternative trophy in time. However, during that year Prestwick persuaded the Royal & Ancient Golf Club and the Honourable Company of Edinburgh Golfers, then based at Musselburgh, to contribute to the cost of a challenge trophy and to help run the championship.

The silver Claret Jug that we recognize today (made by Mackay Cunningham of Edinburgh) was purchased for a sum of £30, and for the next twenty years the championship was played in rotation at Prestwick, St Andrews and Musselburgh, in that order.

Young Tom won the 1872 Open at Prestwick, but in the first Open held at St Andrews the following year, played over two rounds of 18 holes each, his dominance was broken by a local professional, Tom Kidd. At

Musselburgh in 1874 Tom came second again, to a local professional, Mungo Park, but by now he was reported to be suffering from ill health.

In September 1875 Tom and his father played in a Challenge Match at North Berwick, and at the end of the game Young Tom was handed a telegram giving him the news that his wife had been taken seriously ill while giving birth to their first child.

To save time Tom and his father returned by boat across the Firth of Forth, but on arrival at St Andrews he was given the news that both his wife and the baby had died.

Young Tom was heartbroken and never recovered. On Christmas Day, aged just 24, he was found dead in his room by his father.

Old Tom, now based at St Andrews, never played in the Open again, but concentrated on his club-making business and his job as greenkeeper to the Royal & Ancient, a position he held until 1904.

The next few years saw the number of entries increase and in 1885, for the first time, as many as 50 competed. During this time, the time of year that the championship was played varied considerably – sometimes in April when played at Musselburgh, generally in September when played at Prestwick and in October when played at St Andrews.

Between 1877 and 1882 the championship was twice won by the same player on three consecutive occasions, first by Jamie Anderson and then by Bob Ferguson. Anderson, a St Andrews man, started as a caddie and then went on to be a fine club-maker. Ferguson, who also started as a caddie, was from Musselburgh, but after an attack of typhoid in 1883 was never the same golfer again.

Willie Park Jr, son of the first winner in 1860, won two championships in 1887 and again in 1889, the last time the event was held at Musselburgh. Following that he concentrated on golf course architecture and was responsible for Sunningdale Old, Huntercombe and West Hill, among others.

When John Ball triumphed in 1890, at Prestwick, the championship was won for the first time by an Englishman – and an amateur at that. Ball was without doubt one of the finest amateurs of all time. Over 24 years he won the Amateur Championship on eight occasions, a record likely to stand forever.

The Honourable Company of Edinburgh Golfers hosted the 1892 championship and it was held for the first time at their new home, Muirfield, on the shore of the Firth of Forth situated some 20 miles north-east of Edinburgh. This was also the first year that the championship was played over four rounds, and it resulted

RIGHT: *A Vanity Fair caricature of John Ball, one of the finest and most famous amateurs of all time. He won the Amateur Championship a record eight times and the Open Championship in 1890.*

ABOVE: *Harold Hilton, like John Ball, was an amateur from Hoylake. He won the Amateur Championship four times and the Open Championship twice in 1892 and 1897.*

14

RIGHT: *Muirfield photographed at the 1896 Open. J.H. Taylor stands with his hand on his cap whilst Harry Vardon studies his putt on the green of Shelter Hole, the 8th. Vardon then went on to defeat Taylor in a 36-hole play-off.*

in victory for another English amateur, Harold Hilton. Four times Amateur Champion, Hilton has the record of being the only British golfer to have won the US Amateur Championship (1911).

In 1894 the Open left Scotland for the very first time – the venue being the St George's Golf (later known as Royal St George's) Club at Sandwich on the south-east Kent coast. St George's or Sandwich, as the club is affectionately known, had been founded as recently as 1877 and had successfully hosted the Amateur Championship in 1892. The course had developed well and all the leading players travelled south to compete.

This was the beginning of a new era when three players, Harry Vardon, J.H. Taylor and James Braid, dominated the championship. The Great Triumvirate, as they became known, were to win 16 of the 21 Opens played between 1894 and 1914. Taylor was victorious at Sandwich in 1894 and again at St Andrews in 1895, which was also the inaugural year of the US Open. By now prize money for the first place had taken a huge leap to £30.

The Royal Liverpool Golf Club, at Hoylake in Cheshire, was invited to host the 1897 Open. Formed in 1869 Hoylake is one of the oldest clubs in England and Harold Hilton was successful again following his victory at Muirfield in 1892. There followed two victories by Harry Vardon, in 1898 at Prestwick and in 1899 at Sandwich.

By this time a total of 39 Open Championships had been played. In 1860 eight players entered – in 1899 this figure had risen to 101. The Open had changed from a minor local competition held on the west coast of Scotland and watched by a mere handful of spectators, into a truly national event that was watched by thousands.

THE GREAT TRIUMVIRATE
Harry Vardon, James Braid, J.H. Taylor
1900–1914

THESE THREE MEN dominated the game for a period of some twenty years around the turn of the century. Although they were all attached to clubs as professionals, they spent much of their time travelling, playing in exhibition matches, challenge matches and, of course, tournaments.

James Braid was born in Earlsferry, Fife, in February 1870, and Harry Vardon some two months later, on Jersey in the Channel Islands. The following March John Henry (known as J.H.) Taylor was born in Devon. All three men became linked with golf at an early age and by their early twenties were the leading players of their time.

Taylor was the first of the three to win the Open, at Sandwich in 1894, and he won again the following year at St Andrews. Between 1894 and 1914 they won 16 of the 21 Open Championships, Vardon winning an unsurpassed six times, and Taylor and Braid on five occasions. Braid, remarkably, won his five championships in the space of ten years, from 1901 to 1910 and was without doubt the player of the first decade of the century. Taylor and Braid each won twice at St Andrews, an achievement only equalled by Jack Nicklaus in modern times. Their stories will emerge in greater detail in the year-by-year accounts which follow.

LEFT: The Great Triumvirate *painted by Clement Flower in 1913 shows champions J.H. Taylor seated, James Braid looking on and Harry Vardon swinging.*

RIGHT: *A photograph taken at Aberlady prior to the 1906 Open with from right to left: Vardon standing, Taylor, Ted Ray and Braid. Braid preferred rail travel to cars as he suffered from motion sickness.*

1900

Taylor's Third Triumph

$\sim$

APPROPRIATELY THE 1900 Open Championship was played at St Andrews. After a near strike the previous year at Sandwich over prize money, the total sum played for was raised to £125. It was still some way short of the players' demands, but it was at least an improvement.

Warm sunshine greeted the players on the first day but a strong easterly breeze made conditions testing. After two rounds J.H. Taylor led by four strokes following rounds of 79 in the morning and a fine 77 in easier conditions in the afternoon. In second position, on 160, was Harry Vardon, who had won the previous two Opens. Jack White was next on 161, and on 162 was the amateur Mr Robert Maxwell of Tantallon, fresh from his victory in the Challenge Vase at Sandwich. James Braid, who had won the tournament at Musselburgh the previous week, played disappointingly and ended the day on 163, seven strokes off the lead, but certainly not out of contention. Vardon, incidentally, had cut short his stay in the United States to play, and it is likely that the sea voyage and climatic changes would not have helped.

The second day produced much less favourable weather with a heavy sea mist, known in Scotland as a 'haar', occasional showers and a cold north-easterly wind. The championship was effectively over at lunchtime following Taylor's morning round of 78. Vardon could only manage an 80, which left him trailing by six. With such a commanding lead Taylor relaxed and this was reflected in his play – 38 out and home in 37 for a 75, a four-round total of 309 and victory by eight strokes over Vardon, with Braid a further five behind. So the Great Triumvirate occupied the first three places, not for the first time – or the last!

This was Taylor's third triumph in the championship. He had won at his second attempt at Sandwich in 1894 and again at St Andrews the following year.

RIGHT: *Harry Vardon drives from the 1st tee at St Andrews in 1900. His playing partner Sandy Herd looks on from the right with Old Tom Morris on the left. Vardon's bid for the title was thwarted by J.H. Taylor's remarkable golf.*

James Braid Opens His Account

THE CHAMPIONSHIP RETURNED for a third time to Muirfield in 1901 and proved to be another battle between the Great Triumvirate. A record entry of 101 competitors were treated to fine weather, with Muirfield in wonderful condition but with the greens possibly too fast for some. They were described in *The Times* as 'a trifle keen'!

After the first round Vardon led on 77, followed by Willie Park Jr, champion back in 1887 and 1889, on 78, with Braid and Taylor on 79. Braid's score was a fine one considering his first stroke of the day had gone out of bounds.

In the afternoon many of the more prominent players collapsed and the championship was in reality narrowed down to only half a dozen or so competitors. To the great disappointment of the crowd Willie Park's challenge ended following a disastrous 87, due in the main to poor putting. Vardon, remarkably, played the first nine holes in exactly the same numbers as in the morning and was out in 38. A wonderful three at the 17th helped him to a 78 and a share of the lead at the end of the day with Braid. After a disappointing 83 Taylor was seven strokes back in third position.

A large crowd of some three or four thousand travelled in the main from Edinburgh to witness the second and final day. Braid was the crowd's favourite and many followed him. He produced flawless golf and was round in 74. Vardon's challenge faded with a 79, and despite a splendid 74 Taylor still lay seven strokes behind entering the final round.

In the afternoon Braid played conservatively to defend his lead and was round in 80 for a total of 309. News of his score spread and Vardon realized he needed a 75 to tie. Following a first nine of 39 this was still possible, but a six at the 16th ended his hopes and those of his English supporters. A closing 78 left him just three behind Braid, with Taylor third on 313. The gap between the Great Triumvirate and their challengers at the time is shown in that fourth-placed Harold Hilton finished eleven strokes behind Braid and seven behind Taylor.

This was Braid's first Open triumph and the first Scottish success since 1893 when Willie Auchterlonie won at Prestwick. To much acclaim Braid was presented with the Challenge Cup, the Gold Medal and prize money of £50. He was at that time the professional at the Romford Club and had been competing in the championship with moderate success for seven years but this was a breakthrough that saw him dominate the Open for the next decade.

ABOVE: *James Braid pictured in action. His win in 1901 at Muirfield firmly established him as the third member of the Great Triumvirate who dominated the Open Championship for two decades.*

1902

Herd Triumphant with the New Haskell Ball

Tᴴᴇ ʀᴏʏᴀʟ ʟɪᴠᴇʀᴘᴏᴏʟ ᴄʟᴜʙ, ʜᴏʏʟᴀᴋᴇ was the venue for the championship on 4 and 5 June. A record 112 competitors were rewarded with perfect weather conditions on the first day.

The highlight of the first round was without doubt the 72 that Harry Vardon made despite slicing his first two drives out of bounds on the first hole. His score left him with a four-stroke lead over Willie Fernie (76) and a group of several players on 77.

The majority of the crowd followed Vardon in the afternoon and although the Ganton professional could not quite produce the quality of his morning round he played consistently. He was out in 39 and despite a stroke out of bounds at the 16th was home in 38 for a round of 77 and a total of 149. This kept him four strokes ahead of Ted Ray, who had a tremendous afternoon round of 74, and Sandy Herd, who played consistently all day apart from a seven at the 16th in the morning. James Braid, the defending champion, lay one stroke further back after rounds of 78 and 76.

The second and final day produced a strong south-westerly wind that gusted over the links and there were several sharp showers. The scoring was not, therefore, of the exceptionally high level of the previous day, but in three cases remarkable rounds were achieved. One was the 73 of Sandy Herd, which was to turn the championship on its head; the others were the 74s of James Braid and the amateur, James Maxwell.

Vardon could only manage an 80, and therefore his four-stroke lead had turned into a three-stroke deficit. Entering the final round he was effectively the only challenger to Herd, as the next players, Braid, Taylor and his brother Tom Vardon, were a further five strokes behind.

In windy and rain-threatening conditions Herd completed his final round ahead of Vardon in 81 for a total of 307. Vardon played a steady but unspectacular round and stood on the 17th tee requiring two fours to tie. The first was comfortably achieved on the 17th and at the 18th he was on the edge of the green in two and overran the hole with his first putt, leaving his ball some five feet away. With much tension in the air Vardon putted – the ball looked in but at the last moment stopped right on the edge of the hole.

It seemed that the championship was over, but Braid, after a modest outward nine of 40, suddenly produced remarkable golf and with seven fours and two threes played the back nine in 34 to tie Vardon just one stroke behind Herd. Tribute

ᴀʙᴏᴠᴇ: *An advertisement for the new Haskell rubber wound ball which flew better and travelled further. Sandy Herd attributed much of his success at Hoylake to this new ball.*

1902

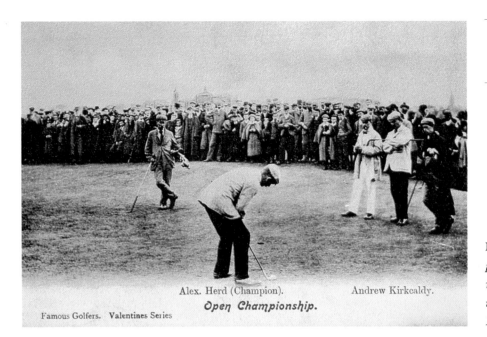

Alex. Herd (Champion).   Andrew Kirkcaldy.

Open Championship.

Famous Golfers.   Valentines Series

LEFT: *Alex 'Sandy' Herd putts his way to Open victory while three times runner-up Andrew Kirkcaldy looks on.*

should be paid to the amateur Robert Maxwell for his closing 74 and the fact that he was the only competitor to break 80 in all four rounds.

So Herd was champion for the first and only time at the age of 34. He went on to be runner-up on no fewer than four other occasions over a period of 28 years. Somewhat overshadowed by Vardon, Braid and Taylor, he was nevertheless a truly great golfer.

Much of Herd's success at Hoylake was attributed to his use of the new rubber-cored Haskell ball. This was a new type of ball that had just been invented by an American from Cleveland, Coburn Haskell. Believing that it must be possible to make a better ball than the gutta percha (or 'guttie' as it was known), Haskell searched for the answer and found it when visiting a friend's rubber factory in Akron, Ohio. He saw some thin rubber strips and had the idea of wrapping them around an elastic core, under tension. Following much experimentation and modification a new ball was produced that consistently flew 20 yards further than the old guttie. Many of the older generation took a while to appreciate its qualities, but after Herd's victory at Hoylake with the ball it became generally accepted. Herd himself had not wanted to use the new-style ball, but after practice rounds with his friend, the amateur John Ball, who was a convert to it, he was persuaded to use it for the championship.

Herd was always considered slightly hot-headed, but late in his career his temperament improved and he won the British Professional Matchplay Championship at the age of 58. Remarkably, aged nearly 70, he played four rounds in a tournament at Moor Park in level fours. In his lifetime he achieved 19 holes in one, 13 of them at Coombe Hill where he served as professional for many years. His elder brother, Fred, was also an accomplished player, winning the US Open in 1898, the first time it was played over 72 holes.

1903

A One-Two Finish for the Vardon Brothers

ABOVE: *Harry Vardon's fourth Open title at Prestwick in 1903 completed a remarkable run in the event: 1st, 6th, 1st, 1st, 2nd, 2nd, 2nd and 1st.*

OF THE 127 ENTRANTS who competed for the 1903 championship at Prestwick, many were undone by the greens which, following days of intense heat, were extremely fast.

Apart from a seven at the 17th in his second round, Harry Vardon played immaculate golf. His rounds of 73 and 77 left him with a lead at the halfway stage of four strokes over Andrew Scott of Elie and five ahead of Jack White of Sunningdale and Willie Hunter of Richmond, who had an excellent second round of 74.

Vardon had recently been ill and had been advised not to play in the championship, but the following day, despite exhaustion, he put together nines of 34 and 38 for a record-equalling 72 and a seven-stroke advantage over Jack White. In the afternoon, confident that an 80 would give him the cup, Vardon played conservatively and was comfortably round in 78 for a total of 300, the lowest aggregate by five strokes since the championship was extended to 72 holes.

A final round of 74 gave Vardon's younger brother Tom second place on his own. For many years overshadowed by the play of his elder brother, Tom Vardon later moved to the St George's Club, Sandwich, and subsequently his game rose to the top level.

So this was Harry Vardon's fourth Open success and his second at Prestwick, where he won in 1898. Soon after his win Vardon fell seriously ill with tuberculosis and spent several months recovering at Mundesley in Norfolk. It would be another eight years before victory in the Open was his again.

TOM VARDON

ALTHOUGH ALWAYS IN THE SHADOW of his brother Harry, Tom Vardon had a fine Open record for some twenty years, on four occasions finishing in the top five. In 1903 he finished second to his brother, but on more than one occasion he finished higher than Harry. As late as 1916 he achieved his best result in the US Open when he came ninth.

Jack White Breaks the 300 Barrier

IN 1904, ROYAL ST GEORGE'S, SANDWICH, was the Open venue for the third time – remarkable for a club that had only been formed in 1877.

The format of the championship altered somewhat, in that it was now held over three days. One round was played on each of the first two days, and two rounds on the third.

Despite the serious illness he had suffered Harry Vardon led at halfway following rounds of 76 and 73. Close on his heels however were many of the leading players of the time: his brother Tom, James Sherlock, Andrew Kirkaldy from St Andrews, Sandy Herd and Willie Park Jr. Some way back on 155 was J.H. Taylor, with James Braid on 157.

On the third morning, however, Braid went to the turn in a staggering 31 strokes (five threes and four fours). A homeward nine of 38 gave him the remarkable total of 69, a score never previously achieved in the championship. To return a score such as this, using the equipment of almost a century ago and given how much course conditions have improved since, was some feat. Vardon meanwhile faded out of the picture following a 79, but Jack White, with a more than respectable 72, was just one behind Braid.

By lunchtime the weather was perfect for links golf and with just a light breeze low scores were expected for the final round. Of the leaders White was first out in the afternoon and, playing wonderful golf from tee to green, was round in 69 (32, 37) for a four-round total of 296, surely a winning score. The two Vardons were next in and neither could mount a serious challenge.

Braid and Taylor meanwhile were still on the course, and on the 18th tee Braid, who had gone to the turn in 34, was told incorrectly that White had finished on 297. Thinking he required a four to tie, he played to the green in two and putted up safely to secure his par and a place in a play-off, or so he thought! (Remember there were no scoreboards on the course in those days.)

Taylor was the last of the potential winners still out on the course and he played unbelievable golf. Standing on the 18th tee he had played just 64 shots and required a birdie three to tie. After two strokes to the edge of the green he rolled his putt up, it touched the lip but rolled on past. And so, after his last-round 68, a record which would stand for many years, Taylor failed by a single stroke and Jack White was champion, having twice before finished runner-up.

With his four-round total of 296, White became the first player to break the 300 barrier for the championship.

BELOW: *Having finished 2nd, 3rd, and 4th in recent years, Jack White's victory in 1904 was well deserved. His four round total smashed the 300 barrier for the first time.*

JACK WHITE.

1905

Braid the Local Hero

THE CHAMPIONSHIP RETURNED to St Andrews, where playing conditions were much more difficult than the previous year at Sandwich, and the winning score was 22 strokes higher.

On the first day the record entry of 152 competitors found conditions especially testing, and in a strong wind and on lightning fast greens no one managed to break 80. Three past champions, Taylor, Vardon and Herd, matched it and Braid, champion in 1901, took 81.

The second day provided kinder weather but still only three scores under 80 were recorded – 77 by Rowland Jones of Wimbledon, 78 by Braid and 79 by James Kinnell of Purley Downs. At the end of the day Jones led on 158, by one from Braid, with Herd, Vardon, Taylor and the Frenchman Arnaud Massy all within seven strokes.

The third and final day dawned with a cool breeze and was a warm and pleasant one for the 45 competitors who had survived the qualifying cut. Old Tom Morris took part for the last time, as the starter on the 1st tee, at the age of 83! Jones's chances were not helped by an eight at the 5th and he completed his morning round in 87. Taylor returned an excellent 78 and, having won the previous two Opens at St Andrews, was now in with a real chance of a third. However, Braid had other ideas and a second 78 left him with a six-stroke cushion entering the afternoon round.

A huge crowd of some four thousand followed their local man and after a front nine of 38 Braid appeared to have the championship in his grasp until the 15th. A drive on to the railway line resulted in a six, and he repeated this at the 16th with his second shot. Two strokes were required to get back on to the fairway, and another six went down on the card. However, two closing fives saw him safely home and Braid was carried from the 18th green shoulder high by his supporters. His last round of 81 left him five strokes ahead of Taylor and Rowland Jones. This was Braid's second success, following his win at Muirfield in 1901, but there was much more to come.

Braid spent many years as a club professional, briefly at Romford, but is better known for his time at Walton Heath where he served for 46 years. A reserved man of few words, Braid became a much sought after course architect and was a highly respected figure among his fellow professionals for whom he did so much to raise their status.

1906

Second Victory at Muirfield for Braid

MUIRFIELD HOSTED ITS fourth Open Championship on 13–15 June 1906.

Three times champion J.H.Taylor, after a disappointing opening 77, returned a remarkable 72 with two nines of 41 and 31! This left him the leader at the halfway stage, one ahead of Vardon and Jack Graham Jr, an amateur from Hoylake. Defending champion James Braid was a further three strokes behind.

On the third and final morning Braid returned a fine 74 and made up one stroke on Taylor, and Rowland Jones, who had done so well the previous year at St Andrews, suddenly came on to the scene with an excellent 73. With one round to play, Taylor still led, on 224 by a single stroke from Jones with Braid two further away.

With closing rounds of 80 and 83 respectively Taylor and Jones's chances were blown away. Vardon could do no better than 78 and this left the route to victory clear for Braid, who required a 76 to win. Out in 38, things looked close, but a long putt for a three on the 17th helped him to secure victory, with a round of 73 and a total of 300, four less than Taylor's score.

So Braid was champion again, for the third time in all and for the second time at Muirfield following his victory there in 1901.

Braid had by now firmly established himself as one of the truly talented golfers alongside his great rivals J.H. Taylor and Harry Vardon. From 1900 to 1910 his record in the Open Championship makes very impressive reading: 3, 1, 2, 5, 2, 1, 1, 5, 1, 2, 1. Few players in the twentieth century dominated a ten year period to such as extent.

RIGHT: *An early and very rare postcard depicting James Braid driving from the 1st tee at Muirfield during the 1906 Open.*

The Claret Jug Goes to France!

1907

HOYLAKE HOSTED the 1907 championship and by this time there were considerable changes made to the qualifying format. The professionals, through the PGA, had been brought into the whole organization of the event more than any time before.

The increased number of entries was causing concern, and it was decided that on the two days preceding the championship all the entrants would play a total of 36 holes in two separate groups. The thirty players with the lowest score in each group would qualify to play in the championship itself. Of the 193 entrants 67, allowing for ties, qualified, and there were some notable non-qualifiers, including 1904 champion Jack White. John Ball Jr, one of Hoylake's more famous amateurs, was to end the week in a creditable 15th position, 17 years after he first triumphed over the Open field at Prestwick in 1890.

After two rounds played in foul weather and a strong wind, any player under 160 was still in with a chance of victory. For example, the 158-yard 4th hole required a full wooden club to reach the green.

Entering the final round it appeared to be a two-horse race, J.H. Taylor leading on 234, one ahead of the Frenchman Arnaud Massy, who had finished fifth and sixth in his only two previous championships in 1905 and 1906. In the final round a seven at the 3rd cost Taylor dearly and he was out in 41. A back nine of 39 saw him home in 80 for a total of 314 but Massy, playing steady golf, went out in 38 and came home in 39 for a total of 312, to become the first overseas player to win the Open.

The success of Massy's career was a story of considerable determination and strength of character, for at the turn of the century it was extremely rare for a Frenchman to play golf. In 1902, aged 25 and with financial backing from supporters at home, Massy travelled to Scotland. He settled down, married a local girl and practised hard at North Berwick. Previously he had played left-handed, simply because in earlier years he had been given a left-handed set, but on arrival in Scotland he learnt to play right-handed! A large, strongly built man, Massy was always at his best when the wind blew.

Four years after his victory at Hoylake he tied with Vardon at Sandwich, conceding at the 35th hole in a play-off. In later years he returned to France, where he became professional at the Chantaco Club. He won the Spanish Open as late as 1927 and 1928, – having just turned fifty – and also won the Open title of his own country on four occasions.

ABOVE: *Arnaud Massy's victory in 1907 was the first win by an overseas player and as yet, the first by a Frenchman.*

1908

Braid by a Distance!

THE 1908 CHAMPIONSHIP was held at Prestwick, but the PGA was keen to add another club to those already on the Open rota. Invitations were sent out to the Royal North Devon Club at Westward Ho! and the Cinque Ports Club (now Royal) at Deal to put forward their credentials. After consideration it was decided that Deal would become the new championship course, and would host the Open in 1909.

After two days of qualifying under another slightly modified system, play got under way, and Ernest Gray from Littlehampton set a scorching pace with a first-round course record of 68. But the bubble soon burst and he followed up with a 79. After rounds of 70 and 72 Braid found himself five strokes ahead of Gray, with David Kinnell of the nearby Prestwick St Nicholas Club and Sandy Herd a further stroke behind.

Despite an eight at the 3rd in the third round Braid somehow managed to go out in 39, and with a round of 77 still held a commanding lead of six strokes over Tom Ball from the West Lancashire Club and Ted Ray from Ganton. In the final round neither managed to stage any sort of challenge to Braid, whose immaculate 72 gave him his fourth championship, by eight strokes. His four record total of 291 comfortably broke the previous record set by Jack White at nearby Sandwich four years earlier.

ABOVE: *James Braid in full swing. He had a long career at Walton Heath Golf Club in Surrey. He moved there in 1904, where he held the position of professional for a remarkable 46 years.*

TOM BALL

BORN IN HOYLAKE in 1882 but not related to John Ball, Tom Ball had a fine Open record in the first few years of the twentieth century, his finest years being 1908 and 1909 when he finished second and third. Despite an unorthodox swing he was renowned as a fine iron player but sadly died in 1919 aged just 37 as a result of war wounds sustained during World War I.

J.H. Taylor – Master of the Cinque Ports

1909

D EAL, JUST A MILE SOUTH-WEST OF SANDWICH, is a typical seaside links, running parallel to the sea and protected from it by a ridge of pebbles. As with most links courses the wind is the determining factor, and when played into the prevailing wind there are few tougher finishing holes.

As well as hosting the championship for the first time in 1909, Deal also saw the birth of an Exhibition area – what we now know as the Tented Village. Manufacturers and retailers showed their wares, and prizes were awarded to those considered to be the best in their category. How different it must have been compared with today's scenes!

After the first day of two rounds J.H. Taylor, having played superb golf from tee to green, led on 147, by a single stroke from the little-known professional from Southdown, Charles Johns. Tom Ball lay a further stroke back, with Braid on 154 after a disappointing first round 79.

On the second day Braid had an excellent 73 but at lunchtime still had six strokes to make up on Taylor following his 74. In the afternoon no one made any serious challenge to Taylor, whose steady and second consecutive 74 left him on 295, four shots clear of Braid and six from Tom Ball. Taylor had, for the moment, reasserted himself as the leading player ahead of Braid.

Overall Deal was considered to be a successful venue, but war would prevent it from hosting another championship until 1920.

RIGHT: *J.H. Taylor makes his winning speech at Deal in 1909. By now he had moved to the Royal Mid Surrey Golf Club in Richmond where he held the position of professional for 40 years before retiring to Westward Ho!*

1910

Braid's Fifth Title in Ten Years

ABOVE: *D & W Auchterlonie display their goods in the Exhibition stand of 1910 at St Andrews. The Auchterlonies are a famous club-making family with connections going back in St Andrews for several generations.*

To commemorate the 50th Open Championship, which was held at St Andrews, a special medal to the value of £10 was added to the £50 first prize. Another change was made to the qualifying system in that there were no qualifying rounds as such, but after the first two rounds only the top 60 players and those tieing would play 36 holes on the final day.

Constant rain fell on the first day of the championship, no play was possible and an extra day was added.

A 17-year-old, George Duncan, originally from Aberdeenshire, led after the first round with an excellent 73. Duncan was also a fine footballer and had rejected an offer to play for Aberdeen as golf was his real passion. He would feature strongly in many more championships, most notably in 1920 at Deal when he was victorious.

The halfway lead was held by Willie Smith, a Carnoustie-born Scot who had become the professional at the New Mexico City Golf Club. At Baltimore in 1899 he had won the US Open. His score of 148 left him a single stroke ahead of Braid and another ahead of Duncan, who had slipped slightly with a 77 in the second round.

However Duncan improved dramatically in the third round and his 71, the lowest score of the week, left him with a three-stroke lead over Braid, whose challenge had faltered slightly with a six at the Road Hole. Imagine how the 17-year-old Duncan must have felt entering the last round of the Open Championship, at the home of golf and with a three-stroke lead over a four-time winner!

Not surprisingly his game fell apart completely and a disastrous 83 was the result, for a total of 304. Smith took 12 more strokes for the last two rounds than the first two and he ended on 308. Sandy Herd made a challenge, going out in 35, but he needed 41 strokes for the back nine and his 76 left him on 303. It was left to Braid, and his last-round 76 gave him a four-round total of 299 and victory by four strokes.

Incredibly, in ten years Braid had won five times and been second three times, and there is no doubting that he was the player of the decade. Although he went on to compete with his two great rivals, Vardon and Taylor, into his mid fifties, this was his last Open success.

He spent many years as a club professional, serving briefly at Romford, then for 46 years at Walton Heath. A reserved, quiet man of few words, Braid became a much sought-after course architect and was a highly respected figure among his fellow professionals, whose status he did so much to raise.

Massy Succumbs to Vardon in Play-Off

1911

~

WITH THE LARGE NUMBER of entrants, 226, problems arose for the 1911 Open at Sandwich in that it was not possible for this number to get round the course twice in two days. Therefore an extra day was added and the players were split into three groups, with the leading 60 playing two further rounds on the final day.

Once this confusing and unsatisfactory qualifying system was over, a wonderful Open Championship followed. A long period of drought had preceded the championship, but rain came just in time to ensure greens in perfect condition.

George Duncan, who had played so well the previous year at St Andrews, led after two rounds on 144. He was followed, four behind, by Ted Ray, Vardon and Taylor. But for the second successive year Duncan had one really poor round, and another disastrous 83 ended his challenge. None of the challengers produced a particularly low score in the third round, and at lunchtime, with one round to play, Vardon was the new leader, three clear of Ray, Arnaud Massy, the 1907 champion, and Braid, the defending champion.

In the afternoon Vardon was the first of the leaders to finish and his disappointing 80 left the door open for his challengers. Some attributed his last round to a change of routine and diet – he had lunched at the club rather than the Guildford Hotel where he was staying! It must be remembered, however, that he had previously been extremely ill and had to take great care of his health.

The amateur, Harold Hilton, champion back in 1892 and 1897, came out of the pack to mount a challenge and stood on the 18th tee requiring a four to tie Vardon. Alas, he needed three strokes to reach the green and his putt to tie shaved the hole but would not drop. Next along came Sandy Herd, and he too needed a four to tie Vardon, but his six-foot putt jumped out of the hole when it seemed in! Massy also required a four to tie, and unlike Hilton and Herd he made no mistake, indeed almost made a three. And so there was a tie, and a play-off over 36 holes took place the following day.

Initially the play-off was close, but by lunch Vardon led by five and this was still the margin when Massy conceded at the 35th. After playing a poor second he threw his club down and advanced towards Vardon with his hand outstretched saying, 'I cannot play this damn game!'

So Vardon was champion for a fifth time – a record that matched that of Braid – and his drought of seven years was over! As for Massy, this was the closest he came to a second title but he continued to play for a further ten years.

ABOVE: *After an eight year gap, Vardon secured his fifth Open title, by way of a 36-hole play-off with Massy – although the game only went as far as the 35th!*

1912

Ted Ray All the Way

ABOVE: *Ted Ray with trilby hat firmly in place. He won the Open in 1912 and won the US Open in 1920. Ray, Harry Vardon and Tony Jacklin remain the only British players to have won both Open titles.*

FOLLOWING MANY MEETINGS and much protestation from the professionals concerning their treatment and the qualifying process, the championship was played at Muirfield on 24 and 25 June. After three days of qualifying in three sections, with each group playing 36 holes on a single day, a field of 62 remained.

Ted Ray, who had finished in the top six in the previous five Opens led after the first day. His 144 left him three ahead of Vardon, with Braid a further stroke behind.

In the third round, with an inward nine of 40, Ray appeared to have left the door open to Braid and Vardon. But Vardon had problems of his own – mainly in bunkers. He took sixes at the 7th, 8th, and 9th holes, having been bunkered on each one. On the 8th he was unlucky when his ball pitched on the green but jumped at right angles, ending in a bunker. Vardon blamed the ball, but others said it hit a stone. The end result was a disastrous 81. Braid too had problems on the greens and he finished in 77.

Only Vardon, with a 71 in the final round, mounted any sort of challenge, and after a steady 75 Ray was champion by four strokes, with a total of 295. No one could deny Ray his victory, which was well deserved after his efforts in previous Open years.

Wearing his battered Homburg hat and with his pipe firmly clenched between his teeth, Ray was a distinctive figure. Having come third after a play-off for the US Open in 1913, he returned to the United States in 1920 and won their championship at Inverness. He, Vardon and Tony Jacklin remain the only British players to have won both Opens.

Ray had moved to the Oxhey club just before his Open success, a move which gave the club instant recognition. He remained there for the rest of his days serving the members in his kindly way and no doubt relieving some of them of their money at billiards, another game in which he excelled!

Coincidentally, Ray was born within a mile of Vardon on the island of Jersey and had followed him as the professional at Ganton.

Taylor's Fifth and Final Title

1913

⁓

THE 1913 OPEN SAW THE START of the 'international invasion' of overseas players. From America came John McDermott, holder of the US Open, and Tom Macnamara. From France, as well as Massy, Jean Gassiat and Louis Teller travelled over to compete. In all a record 269 players entered for the 1913 Open at Hoylake. With such a large entry, qualifying was again played in three sections over three days, the leading 20 in each group going on to play in the championship proper. The major casualty in qualifying was George Duncan, who missed the cut by four strokes.

After the first day of two rounds Ted Ray, the defending champion, led J.H. Taylor by a single stroke. Vardon on 154 was seven strokes off the lead. A gale force wind blew on the second and final day and this strongly favoured Taylor, who hit the ball on a much lower trajectory than Ray. A 77 to Ray's 81 left him three strokes ahead entering the afternoon's final round.

A wobbly start to his round saw Taylor take 41 strokes to the turn. However, two incidents were to secure him his fifth Open success. Taylor holed a pitch shot of some 50 yards at the 14th for an eagle three, and almost simultaneously Ray took an eight on the 490-yard 3rd. Ray never recovered and took a disastrous 84 for a total of 312. Taylor was victor by eight strokes. His compact swing had held together in the wind and rain, while his fellow competitors had succumbed to the appalling conditions. He had, however, come very close to not qualifying in the first place, having to hole a six-foot putt on the final green. The leading overseas player was John McDermott, who finished in fifth place.

Taylor, who was a highly-strung and emotional man, considered his victory of 1913 to be some of the best golf he ever played. Although this was his final win, he did come second the following year and as late as 1924, aged 53, he came fifth. It was remarkable that all five of his Open victories were achieved with several strokes in hand.

In 1950 Taylor was elected an honorary member of the R&A, and in 1961 on his 90th birthday the captain and past captains presented him with a silver salver bearing their signatures. In retirement he settled at his beloved Westward Ho! where from his house on a hill above the course he would sit, looking through his binoculars at the links that had given him so much pleasure over a long and distinguished career.

The renowned writer Bernard Darwin said of him: 'He turned a feckless company into a self-respecting and respected body of men.'

ABOVE: *J.H. Taylor's fifth and final victory at Hoylake. This win was considered by many, including himself, to be his best.*

1914

Sixth Title for Vardon. A Record for All Time?

ABOVE: *A fine example of Harry Vardon using the interlocking or 'Vardon grip' as it became known. He was attributed with being the first player to use the grip but some say that the twice Amateur Champion Johnny Laidlay was in fact its creator.*

AFTER TAYLOR'S SUCCESS THE PREVIOUS YEAR the Great Triumvirate had now won five Open titles each and they were all at Prestwick vying for a record sixth. After two rounds the lead was with Vardon following rounds of 73 and 77. He had a narrow advantage of one stroke over James Ockenden and was two ahead of Taylor.

Vardon and Taylor were paired together for the final day and they were followed by huge crowds, thought to be in excess of five thousand. In the morning Taylor took command, and his 74 to Vardon's 78 gave him a two-stroke lead. Ockenden had had his day and was to challenge no more.

Early in the fourth round Taylor extended his lead to three strokes, but after a wet and disastrous seven at the water-lined fourth he dropped further strokes at the 8th, 9th, 10th and 11th holes. A three-stroke lead had in ten holes turned into a deficit of five. He struggled on bravely, but his closing 83 let in Vardon for his record sixth victory at the age of 44.

This marked the end of the dominance of the Great Triumvirate and although they all continued to play for many years, war brought an abrupt halt to the Open Championship.

Vardon had an enormous influence on the game. When he first appeared his notably upright swing, though rhythmic and graceful, surprised many who were more used to a sweeping stroke with a wider arc. He also made popular the overlapping grip, in which the little finger of the right hand overlaps the index finger of the left. This eventually became known as the Vardon Grip, although the amateur player Johnny Laidlay is thought to have been the actual originator of this famous grip.

Vardon had initially learnt his golf on the island of Jersey, where he was born, and it was on the advice of his younger brother Tom that he went to Ripon in Yorkshire in 1890. He soon moved on to Bury and in 1896 became the professional at Ganton, again in Yorkshire. At the US Open in 1920 and now aged 50, Vardon tied for second place, having been five strokes ahead with seven titles to play. However, a sudden gale and tiredness were his undoing and a 78 left him a single stroke behind fellow Briton Ted Ray.

From 1903 until his death in 1937 Vardon was based at the South Herts club in North London.

Few people can be said to have had more influence on the game of golf than Harry Vardon.

THE GOLDEN YEARS
1920-1933

FOLLOWING THE END OF WAR it was decided not to hold the Open in 1919; instead a tournament, The Professional Golfers Championship, was held at St Andrews in June.

In 1920 the Open resumed and was held for a second time at The Royal Cinque Ports Club at Deal. The Great Triumvirate had by now won all of their 16 championships. Taylor, still a stern competitor, was not quite the player he had been, and Vardon, although he had tied second in the 1920 US Open, now aged 50 would never again challenge seriously in the Open. Braid likewise had had his day, although he would finish runner-up in the British Matchplay Championship as late as 1927.

The 1920s saw the arrival of a new era of professionals who would dominate the next few years, but there were two in particular who stood out. They were two of the most glamorous and exciting sportsmen of their time and are still two of the most talked-about golfers in history, and they were both American.

In the space of nine years Walter Hagen, with four wins, and Bobby Jones, with three, had a stranglehold on the championship. Hagen had already made a name for himself at home, having won the 1914 US Open aged just 21. In 1930 Jones achieved what was considered impossible, winning the Amateur and Open Championships of Britain and America. His year of glory will be dealt with in more detail later.

Two other Americans would stamp their presence on the championship: Tommy Armour, an 'American Scot', and Gene Sarazen. Again we shall hear more of them in later pages. This American invasion was to add a new dimension to the championship and make it a truly international event.

RIGHT: *Bobby Jones drives from the 17th tee at St Andrews en route to his record breaking score of 285 in 1927. Note the old railway line to the left.*

1920

George Duncan Recovers from Two 80s to Win the Open

Tʜᴇ ᴏᴘᴇɴ ᴡᴀs ɴᴏ ʟᴏɴɢᴇʀ ᴀ ɴᴀᴛɪᴏɴᴀʟ ᴇᴠᴇɴᴛ – it had become an international one – and in 1919 the Royal & Ancient had been asked to take control of its management.

With the increase in recent years of crowds, car parking, the Tented Village and grandstands, it is difficult to imagine Deal coping with an Open Championship. It is better known as a venue for amateur championships. Nevertheless in 1920 it saw one of the more remarkable days in Open history. After two rounds Abe Mitchell, often described as the best golfer at the time never to win the Open, led the field by six shots and led George Duncan by 13. By the end of the third round all 13 strokes had gone following Duncan's 71 and Mitchell's disastrous 84! Duncan's sudden change in fortune was attributed to his purchase of a new driver in the Exhibition Tent following two rounds of 80.

Mitchell had arrived at the course just as Duncan was holing out for his 71, and one can only surmise that nerves got the better of him. On the 1st green he had an 18-inch putt for his par – and left it six inches short!

To his credit, although shattered by the experience of the morning, Mitchell recovered slightly with a closing 76, but this still left him only in fourth place on 307, one behind Ted Ray, two behind the 52-year-old Sandy Herd and four behind Duncan, whose closing 72 completed four extraordinary rounds of 80, 80, 71 and 72.

This was Duncan's only Open success, but he challenged for many more years and regularly finished in the top half dozen. One of the quickest players ever seen, Duncan had many other successes, most notably two wins over Hagen, once by 6 and 5 at Wentworth and again when captaining the winning Ryder Cup team at Moortown in 1929, this time by the embarrassing margin of 10 and 8 over 36 holes.

Aʙᴇ Mɪᴛᴄʜᴇʟʟ

Oᴠᴇʀ ᴀ ᴘᴇʀɪᴏᴅ ᴏғ ᴛᴡᴇɴᴛʏ ʏᴇᴀʀs *Mitchell finished in the top five on five occasions. Part of a famous Sussex golfing family, he was often described as the finest player not to win the title. In 1920 he led the field by six strokes after two rounds but a disastrous third round 84 (put down to nerves) was his undoing.*

Aʙᴏᴠᴇ: *Open Champion George Duncan displays a full shoulder turn. One of the game's fastest players, his victory at Deal in 1920 was remarkable as he trailed Abe Mitchell at the halfway stage by 13 strokes but closing rounds of 71 and 72 saw him in as champion with two strokes to spare.*

Hutchison in the Groove at St Andrews

THE CHAMPIONSHIP RETURNED to St Andrews in 1921 and unlike previous years all the qualifying was held immediately before the championship at St Andrews itself. A total of 152 competitors entered and 85 qualified for the championship proper.

Jock Hutchison, born in St Andrews in 1884, but based from an early age in the United States, had sailed to Britain early in the year and played dozens of rounds on the Old Course in preparation. His efforts were rewarded with an opening round of 72, which included a hole in one at the 8th and almost another at the short par-four 9th when his tee shot missed the pin by inches. After a second round of 75 he held a two-stroke lead over defending champion George Duncan.

On the third and final day a 79 left Hutchison one behind the hugely talented British amateur, Roger Wethered, with one round to play, but four behind joint leaders Sandy Herd and fellow American Jim Barnes. In his third round of 72 Wethered had incurred a penalty stroke when walking backwards and treading on his ball at the 14th. How expensive could that have been? He returned an excellent 71 in the fourth round but crucially dropped a stroke at the final hole.

Meanwhile Herd and Barnes both had disastrous 80s and it was left to Hutchison to complete the story. He produced a marvellous 70, a great score in the circumstances, and he and Wethered were tied. Wethered needed some persuading to stay on for the 36 hole play-off as he was supposed to be playing in a cricket match in the south the next day! He did of course, but to no avail, and his chance of becoming only the third amateur at the time to win the Open after Harold Hilton and John Ball was denied him. The play-off was won by Hutchison with 150 to Wethered's 159.

The crowd at St Andrews had been astonished by the amount of backspin Hutchison could put on the ball, and irons such as his with deep square grooves were soon banned. His victory, which followed his triumph in the 1920 US PGA Championship, was the first by an American – albeit an adopted one – at the Open. Later he was a dominant force on the American Seniors Tour and for many years in the 1960s played in the opening group to start the Masters at Augusta.

Wethered, meanwhile, went on to achieve great things in the amateur game. He won the Amateur Championship in 1923, played in five Walker Cup teams and was Captain of the Royal & Ancient in 1946.

It was at this championship that a young Bobby Jones tore up his card in the third round. Having taken 46 to the turn and then sixes at the 10th and 11th, he had had enough!

BELOW: *Hutchison's victory of 1921 was the first by an American – although he was born in Scotland! It also heralded the beginning of a period of domination by American players.*

1922

Duncan's Last-Round 69
Not Enough to Stop Hagen

THE CHAMPIONSHIP COMMITTEE had decided that the venue for coming championships would in future be fixed two years in advance rather than the yearly system that had been in place. It was also decided that the championship should always be held on a links course, as indeed to date it always had been.

Qualifying took place at the neighbouring Kentish courses of Princes and at Royal St George's, where the event proper was held on 22 and 23 June. It was the fifth occasion in 26 years that this gem of a course on the south-east Kent coast had been used.

Walter Hagen, Gene Sarazen and Jim Barnes all travelled over, as did Jock Hutchison to defend his title.

Incredibly, after the first round J.H. Taylor, now aged 53, shared the lead with Ted Ray on 73. Barnes, an American but born in Cornwall was on 75, with George Duncan and Hagen on 76. In the next round, however, Taylor slipped to 78 and lost the lead to Hagen.

Following a third round of relatively high scoring at least half a dozen players could still win. Hagen finished with a fine 72 and the only person left out on the course who could catch him was the champion of two years earlier, George Duncan. He was playing what his friends called 'crazy golf'. At seven o'clock in the evening he stood on the last tee needing a birdie three to win. After a perfect drive he played a spoon (four-wood), which on reaching the green broke left and settled in a grassy hollow, later named after him. A chip and putt would tie him with Hagen, but alas he could not manage it and despite Duncan's heroic 69 Hagen became champion by a single stroke.

Presumably nobody was more relieved than the reporters who, wishing to be the first to reveal the result, had rushed into Sandwich to send the news of Hagen's victory to the United States as soon as he had completed his round! There was reason enough for their excitement. This was the first time a native-born American had won the championship.

LEFT: *Walter Hagen putting out on the final green at Royal St George's, en route to winning the first of his four Open titles.*

Havers Keeps Hagen at Bay – Just!

1923

~

ABOVE: *Troon's first Open in 1923 brought victory for Englishman Arthur Havers but this was the last time home crowds would celebrate a home victory for ten years.*

For the first time the championship moved to the delightful setting of Troon, just north of Prestwick, in Ayrshire, on the west coast of Scotland. Formed in 1878 Troon has had many famous names involved with its layout, notably the 1883 Open Champion Willie Fernie (he was also the club's professional), James Braid, Dr Alistair MacKenzie of Augusta fame and Frank Pennink. Troon would host the Open on six further occasions in the century and come to be regarded as one of the great links courses with one of the toughest finishes in golf.

Hagen returned to defend his title and came within inches of doing so, but he was thwarted by a young Englishman, Arthur Havers, the professional at Coombe Hill. Two years previously Havers had missed out by just three strokes when Hutchison won the championship at St Andrews and, incredibly, nine years earlier had qualified for the Open at the age of 16.

Havers played three steady rounds of 73, which left him one stroke ahead of the Australian Joe Kirkwood, two ahead of Hagen and three ahead of an American who would nearly win the title twice more, MacDonald Smith.

Kirkwood became famous all over the world for his trick shots and it was said, rather unkindly, that the only thing he could not do was hit one dead straight! During his career he did win the Opens of Australia, New Zealand and Canada, but never quite clinched the Open. He was a remarkable man who on Christmas Day 1960, aged 63, went round his home course in 62! It was estimated that in all he played 6,470 courses world-wide!

Kirkwood finished with a disappointing 78, Havers a 'safe' 76 and MacDonald Smith a 75. It was left to Hagen, who required a 73 to win and ultimately a birdie three at the last to tie. His second was sliced into a bunker just in front of the clubhouse windows. In true Hagen style he had the flag removed, but it was too much to ask. His ball ran up close to the hole, but Havers was champion with a stroke to spare. Havers had a calm exterior but inside he was a very determined player. Renowned for the precision of his iron play, he also represented Great Britain and Ireland on three occasions in the Ryder Cup including the victorious year of 1933 when he won both his matches.

This was the last time the British could celebrate an Open Champion for many years. A golden period for America was dawning, and a home victory would not be seen again until 1934, when Henry Cotton finally broke a sequence of ten American victories.

1924 *Hagen the Showman Does It Again!*

FROM AN ENTRY of 276, there was a total of 86 qualifiers for the 1924 championship at the Royal Liverpool Club, Hoylake.

Walter Hagen had taken 83 in the first qualifying round and was in danger of not playing in the championship at all. But qualify Hagen did, and he continued to be the game's great showman. He and Sarazen were both staying at the Adelphi Hotel in Liverpool and on one occasion they emerged together at the same time that a crowd had gathered to see the Lord Mayor in his robes of office. It did not occur to Hagen that the small platform in place could be there for anyone but himself, and he calmly mounted it and waved appreciatively to the gathered crowd!

Ernest Whitcombe was the eldest of three sons of a greenkeeper from Burnham in Somerset and had learnt his game on its windswept sandhills. At the halfway stage his scores of 77 and 70 left him two ahead of the veteran J.H. Taylor and three ahead of Hagen and MacDonald Smith. After the third round Hagen had clawed back that deficit, and when Whitcombe took 43 to the turn in the last round it looked as though his chance of glory had gone. But suddenly his game returned and a homeward nine of 35 restored his hopes.

Hagen, despite poor driving, kept in the hunt thanks to the remainder of his game. The championship ended with him needing to hole a putt of nine or ten feet on the 72nd green for victory – which he did with apparent nonchalance.

As he left the final green a newspaper correspondent said to him: 'You appeared to take that putt very casually, Hagen. Did you know you had it to win?'

'Sure I knew I had it to win,' said Hagen, 'but no man ever beat me in a play-off!' – which was completely untrue as he had lost the previous year's US PGA in a play-off against Gene Sarazen!

So Walter Hagen had secured his second Open Championship, to go with his two US Open triumphs of 1914 and 1919 – but there was much more to come!

LEFT: *Walter Hagen is congratulated by his wife after winning at Hoylake in 1924. A first round 83 in qualifying almost eliminated him but in true Hagen style he bounced back to take the title.*

RIGHT: *A gathering of Open champions: back row, left to right: Harry Vardon, James Braid, Sandy Herd, Jack White and Arnaud Massy. Front row, left to right: George Duncan, Walter Hagen, Jim Barnes and Ted Ray.*

Farewell to Prestwick Where It All Began

1925

~

PRESTWICK IS A FAST RUNNING COURSE, with bumpy fairways, deep bunkers and many blind shots, sometimes played in unpredictable winds. It is also on the small side, and by now the event was outgrowing the restricted area in which the course is set. For this reason when the championship returned to its original home for the first time since 1914, it was to be for the final time.

ABOVE: *Jim Barnes's win at Prestwick sealed victory in all the then Majors, having won the first two US PGA titles in 1916 and 1919 and the US Open in 1921.*

Hagen did not cross the Atlantic to defend his title, and the main American challenge lay with Jim Barnes and MacDonald Smith. At last it looked as though MacDonald Smith was to win his first Major trophy, having been runner-up in the US Open as far back as 1910, and having finished third in the previous two Opens. On 221 after three rounds, he led by five strokes from Barnes and Archie Compston and by seven from Ted Ray and Abe Mitchell.

Barnes was out early in the final round and quietly made his way round the course, avoiding the huge crowds who were waiting to watch the Carnoustie-born Smith on his march to victory. His round of 74 was a fine effort but it left Smith requiring just 78 to win or 79 for a tie. But chaotic crowd behaviour completely ruined his game and he fell away to finish with a disastrous 82 and fourth place, three behind Barnes and two behind Compston and Ray. If ever there was an Open that was lost rather than won, this final championship at Prestwick was the one.

Although Smith continued for many years as one of the world's leading players and went on to finish second in the championship twice more, this had been his best chance of victory. The effects of his failure to take it were deep and lasting.

Jim Barnes was a fine player who had learnt his game at an early age in Cornwall, where he was the assistant professional at the Lelant Golf Club. Aged 19 he emigrated to the United States and won the US PGA title in both 1916 and 1919 and the US Open in 1921 as well as this Open title of 1925.

Probably the tallest man ever to win a Major championship, Barnes was a quiet, methodical man who, although a naturalized American, was always proud of his English birth.

MACDONALD SMITH

*F*ROM A FAMOUS GOLFING FAMILY *in Carnoustie, Smith emigrated to the United States and has the reputation for being possibly the finest player never to win a Major championship. His record of near misses in the Open and US Open was remarkable. Second in the Open in 1930 and 1932, his most notable collapse was in 1925 when a last-round 78 at Prestwick would have given him victory. However, vast and over-enthusiastic crowds upset him and he fell away with a disastrous 84. Despite this Smith remained a fine player and a most popular one. It could be said that he was unfortunate to be at his peak at the same time as Jones, Hagen and Sarazen!*

FRED ROBSON

A fine club-maker and coach, Robson was attached to the Addington club in Surrey for many years. *A veteran of the Open from 1908 for some 25 years, he finished in the top five on four occasions. Twice he finished just behind Bobby Jones, and on another occasion he was fourth behind Walter Hagen.*

THE WHITCOMBE FAMILY

A REMARKABLE GOLFING FAMILY *from Burnham in Somerset, the three Whitcombe brothers played regularly in Open Championships between 1914 and 1948. Ernest, the eldest, was second to Walter Hagen in 1924 and fourth in 1927. The middle brother, Charles, finished in the top ten on eight occasions, and Reg, the youngest brother, had a wonderful record, coming second to Henry Cotton at Carnoustie before taking the title in horrendous weather conditions the following year at Sandwich.*

The Year of Great Change and Jones's Miracle Shot

1926

1926 PROVED TO BE A YEAR of radical change. The championship was played for the first time at the Lytham (now Royal Lytham) and St Annes Club on the Lancashire coast. The club had been inspected in 1923, accommodation was more than adequate and accessibility was considered excellent. Although it was slightly shorter and possibly inferior to some of the other championship courses, its greens were seen as being of superb quality.

The second change was in the method of qualifying. It was decided that three regional events would take place, in the north, the south and central England. Entrants from overseas were to be distributed equally between the central and southern sections and amateurs were to play in the section in which their home club was located. After just one year this system was deemed a failure and for the 1927 championship the old method of qualifying was restored.

The last and most significant change was the introduction of gate money. In previous years the funds to run the event, including prize money, had been found through entry fees and subscriptions from the host clubs. Introduction of gate money at the Amateur earlier in the year had been a success, predominately because it reduced the number of 'undesirable' spectators.

Bobby Jones had travelled over to play in the Amateur Championship at Muirfield, where he lost in the fifth round to Scottish golfer Andrew Jamieson without winning a hole. Following that he defeated Cyril Tolley 12 and 11 in the Walker Cup singles at St Andrews and then had to move south to Sunningdale for the Open qualifying. In his first round he played the nearest thing to the perfect round of golf, his two nines of 33 on the Old Course containing nothing higher than a four. His second round was a mere 68!

In the championship itself a week later Hagen started with a 68, then spoiled his chances with a 77, and after two rounds Jones shared the lead with fellow American 'Wild' Bill Mehlhorn.

On the third and final day Hagen and Mehlhorn fell further back and by the afternoon round the destiny of the title lay between Jones and his playing partner, fellow American Al Watrous. Watrous had scored a tremendous 69 in the morning to give himself a two-stroke lead, and with five holes to play in the afternoon this was still the difference. By the time they reached the 17th tee Jones had clawed the two strokes back and they were level.

It was now that Jones played perhaps one of the most outstanding and famous shots in golfing history. With Watrous on the green in two, Jones faced a shot of

BELOW: *The plaque erected to commemorate Bobby Jones's remarkable stroke to Royal Lytham's 17th green.*

1926

RIGHT: *The legendary Bobby Jones at Hoylake with the Dee Estuary in the background. This was painted by J.A.A. Berrie.*

some 170 yards from a flat lie in a bunker with nothing but gorse and scrub between him and the green. He chose a mashie-niblick (equivalent to a modern-day eight or nine-iron). His contact was clean and the ball flew straight to the heart of the green, ending inside his opponent's.

Visibly stunned, Watrous three-putted. Jones made his four, and with a four to a five at the last he was champion by two strokes.

Hagen finished two strokes further back, and this was to be the one and only championship in the British Isles where he and Jones competed against each other. It should be stressed that despite his last-round 78 Watrous was also a fine player, whose victory in the Canadian Open in 1922 was just one of 34 tournament wins.

Jones returned home and two weeks later won the US Open, which was unusually late that year – normally it preceded the Open. The club with which he made his miracle shot still hangs in the clubhouse at Lytham and a plaque to commemorate the stroke can be seen on the 17th hole.

It is ironic to think that Jones only played in the championship because of his poor performance in the Amateur. Had he won that, his plans were to travel home before the Open!

Jones Again from Start to Finish   1927

OLLOWING THE DRAMA of the previous year at Lytham the championship returned to St Andrews with just a few alterations following the radical changes of 1926.

The old method of qualifying was restored, with rounds being played over the New and Old Courses on the two days preceding the championship. The format of 100 players qualifying, a cut being made after two rounds and the championship taking place over three days was retained.

Entry fees reverted to £1 for professionals and £2 for amateurs! However, St Andrews being a difficult course to seal off and there being a surplus of funds left over from Lytham, no gate money was charged. The total purse was £275 with, for the first time, a prize of £100 on offer to the winner.

The event itself was effectively over early on, with Jones leading from start to finish. His first-round 68 was a course record that included several enormous putts. No one could get near him, and further rounds of 72, 73 and 72 left him as champion by six strokes from Jersey-born Aubrey Boomer and Fred Robson, a renowned club-maker and coach, then the professional at Cooden Beach but latterly for many years at Addington.

Having torn up his card in frustration at the previous St Andrews Open in 1921, Jones had wanted this championship more than anything. The crowd's affection for him as a man and their admiration of him as a golfer were evident as he was carried shoulder high from the 18th green.

LEFT: *Amid ecstatic crowds, Bobby Jones is carried from the 18th green following his Open victory at St Andrews in 1927. Already a national hero in the United States, the British golfing public had now taken him to their hearts.*

1928   *Hagen – The Prince of Sandwich*

～

THE OPEN MOVED SOUTH AGAIN to Royal St George's in Kent, and this time anyone wishing to see the golfing greats such as Hagen and Sarazen in action had to pay! Gate money was reintroduced and would become a permanent feature.

Walter Hagen's preparations for the championship had not been encouraging. The day after arriving in England he started a 72-hole match against Archie Compston at Moor Park. Without doubt he had not acclimatized, and his play reflected this as he lost 18 and 17!

By the time he arrived at Sandwich he was back on form but at the halfway stage the lead lay with José Jurado, the first Argentinian professional to make an impact on the game. This genial, dapper little man with a lightning quick swing had come eighth at Lytham in 1926, and at Sandwich following rounds of 74 and 71 he led Sarazen and Hagen by two. Sadly he fell away with closing scores of 76 and 80, but he would be back – much more was to be heard of him at Carnoustie in 1931.

LEFT: *Hagen and Archie Compston before the start of their 72-hole match at Moor Park preceding the 1928 Open. Hagen lost by the embarrassing margin of 18 and 17 but it was a different story by the time they arrived at Sandwich.*

1928

LEFT: *It's all smiles from Hagen as he lifts the Claret Jug and celebrates his third Open title and his second success at Royal St George's.*

The title was contested between the two Americans, and Hagen's two closing 72s to Sarazen's 73s gave him his third Open success and his second at Sandwich. The Prince of Wales (the future Edward VIII), who was the Captain of the club and an avid player himself, had followed Hagen throughout his last round and later presented him with the Claret Jug. Theirs was to become a long and close friendship.

Archie Compston, regularly a high finisher in the championship, had another good week and finished just one stroke behind Sarazen, with Percy Alliss joint fourth.

Sarazen will always consider this a championship that he could or even should have won. The seven he took at the Canal hole, the 14th, in the second round, and a six on the very last hole did not help his cause.

ARCHIE COMPSTON

A TALL, AGGRESSIVE personality, Compston was a regular Open contender from 1920 for some 25 years. Although second to Jim Barnes at the last Prestwick Open in 1925, he will be remembered for his 18 and 17 victory against Walter Hagen over 72 holes in 1928 preceding the Open at Sandwich. There Hagen got his revenge and took the title from Sarazen, with Compston finishing third. At Hoylake in 1930 a third round 68 gave him a one stroke lead but a disastrous last round 82 let in Bobby Jones to take the title.

1929 | *Hagen's Fourth Title – By a Mile*

BELOW: Hagen escapes from sand en route to securing his fourth and final Open title. His four round 282 total left him six strokes clear of his nearest rival, fellow American Johnny Farrell.

Tʜᴇ ᴇɴᴛɪʀᴇ ᴜs ʀʏᴅᴇʀ ᴄᴜᴘ ᴛᴇᴀᴍ gathered with 99 other competitors at Muirfield for the 1929 Open. In addition to the Claret Jug they played for an increased purse of £400, with prize money being paid to the top 23 finishers, the winner receiving £100.

Percy Alliss continued his fine form of 1928 and led following a 69, but sadly fell away with further scores of 76, 76 and 79 – still good enough to leave him in joint fourth place for the second consecutive year.

At the halfway stage the current US PGA champion, Leo Diegel, led on 140. Hagen, after an extraordinary second-round 67, a course record, was on 142, and five strokes back was the then US Open champion, Johnny Farrell.

RIGHT: Legendary golf writer and accomplished amateur Bernard Darwin in conversation with visiting American golfers Johnny Farrell (middle) and Gene Sarazen (right).

ABOVE: *Henry Cotton congratulates Walter Hagen on his second round 67 as they leave the 18th green at Muirfield.*

But on the last day it was all Hagen. In far from ideal conditions Diegel returned 82 and 77, while Hagen's two 75s left him on 292 and six strokes clear of Farrell.

Hagen returned to the British Isles on many more occasions but this was his last Open success. He was a true showman, a real champion and lived like a king. One of his more famous quotes was: 'Never hurry, never worry, and always remember to smell the flowers along the way.' Another was: 'I never wanted to be a millionaire, I just wanted to live like one.' Walter Hagen certainly did both!

Bobby Jones once remarked that he loved to play golf with Hagen, saying, 'He goes along, chin up, smiling away, never grousing about his luck, playing the ball as he finds it.'

It was also Hagen who was largely responsible for the change in status of professional golfers as a whole. As Gene Sarazen said, 'All the professionals who have a chance to go after the big money today should say a silent thanks to Walter each time they stretch a cheque between their fingers.'

At Muirfield, in true Hagen style, he handed over to his caddie, Ernest Hargreaves, his winner's cheque for £100 – an enormous amount of money at the time for a 16-year-old.

With four Open titles, two US Open titles and five US PGA titles, Hagen ranks second behind Jack Nicklaus in the number of major titles won. He also captained the first US Ryder Cup team to win in Britain in 1937, having already played in six previous matches.

1930

The Year of the 'Impossible' Grand Slam

~

WHEN BOBBY JONES RETURNED to the United Kingdom in 1930 after a gap of two years his immediate target was not a third Open success (that could come later), but the Amateur Championship held at St Andrews.

This he achieved on Saturday, 31 May – despite one or two close shaves along the way. In the third round he beat Cyril Tolley only at the 19th, having halved the 17th in four after his ball appeared to bounce off a spectator at the back of the green. It is reputed that a crowd of some twelve thousand had watched this match! In his semi-final against fellow American George Voight he won by a single hole despite being two down with five to play. However, he was never in trouble in the 36-hole final against Roger Wethered, winning by 7 and 6. His dream had come true and the first leg of the 'impossible' Grand Slam had been achieved. And so on to Hoylake for the Open.

After two rounds Jones led by a single stroke, but in the first three holes of the third round he dropped eight strokes to par! It is difficult to imagine a player of his quality doing such a thing, but to his credit he recovered to finish with a 74. This left him trailing Archie Compston by a single stroke after his fine 68, with Leo Diegel two further back.

But disaster befell Compston in the final round. He started with fives and sixes, worse followed, and an 82 left him way down the field six strokes away. Jones meanwhile started well enough, but at the long 8th, when just off the green in two, he took a further five strokes to complete the hole – again difficult to imagine!

RIGHT: *Jones drives from the 2nd tee at Hoylake. With half of the 'Grand Slam' in the bag he returned home to take the US Open the following month and then amazingly went on to win the US Amateur.*

1930

LEFT: *Bobby Jones receives the trophy at Hoylake following his two stroke victory over Carnoustie-born but naturalised American player MacDonald Smith.*

However, Jones gritted his teeth and ground out the remaining holes to finish in 75. Diegel too took 75 and MacDonald Smith 71, but they were both two more than Jones's four-round total of 291. Having only played what he described as 'average' golf, Jones was champion for a third time and the second leg of the Grand Slam was complete.

He moved on to Interlachen in July for victory in the US Open, and the 'impossible' was achieved at the Merion Cricket Club on 27 September when he comfortably won the US Amateur.

The son of an Atlanta lawyer, Bobby Jones was sick and weak as a baby and there were doubts about his survival. But survive he did; by the age of five he was playing the game, and by 14 he was good enough to make the quarter-finals of the US Amateur. At 21 he won the first of his four US Opens, and he also won the US Amateur on five occasions.

Aged just 28 at the time of the 'Grand Slam', he retired from competitive golf, having achieved all there was to achieve, in order to concentrate on his legal practice. The strain of competitive golf had taken its toll on his health, and in major events he had found it difficult to keep food down, sometimes losing as much as a stone in weight.

Jones's dream was to build his own course where he and his friends could play in peace, and he was instrumental in the birth of the Augusta National Club and the US Masters.

Sadly, in the 1950s he developed a muscular disease that was to cripple him completely, but throughout he never complained or lost his courage or courtesy.

It is not just for his golfing records that Jones will be remembered. He was a true amateur – without doubt the greatest there has ever been – and his contribution to the game through his insistence on preserving its traditional sporting ethos remains enormous.

The respect felt for Jones in the game was shown when he was given the freedom of the Burgh of St Andrews in 1958 and when, following his death in 1971, a service was held in the town to celebrate his life. In addition, the 10th hole on the Old Course bears his name and a fine portrait hangs in the Royal & Ancient clubhouse as a memorial to him.

1931

The 'Silver Scot' Returns Home to Victory

BELOW: *Tommy Armour receiving the Open trophy from the Earl of Airlie at Carnoustie. Following his US Open win in 1927, his later success in the US PGA completed victory in all of the then Major Championships.*

THE UNITED STATES were again strongly represented when the Open was played for the first time at Carnoustie in 1931.

Just a few miles across the Tay estuary from St Andrews, Carnoustie has records to confirm the existence of golf there since 1560. Allan Robertson, the first of the great early professionals, laid out ten holes between 1839 and 1842. The course was extended to 18 holes by Old Tom Morris in 1867 and slightly revamped in 1926 by James Braid. Carnoustie offers one of the world's great challenges, and as with most links courses it is the wind that really makes the difference.

After three rounds the Argentinian, José Jurado, who three previously had had a great chance to win at Sandwich, led by three strokes from MacDonald Smith, another who had such a great opportunity in 1925. Two strokes further back were Americans Tommy Armour and Gene Sarazen and the British

professional Percy Alliss. Henry Cotton, the new young hope of England, had led with Jurado, but a third-round 79 put him out of contention. However, it would not be long before he experienced victory.

The first player to make a challenge in the afternoon was Armour, who was the current US PGA champion. His record-equalling 71 gave him a total of 296, but his miserable expression showed that he for one felt it was not good enough.

Alliss and Sarazen went on to complete 73s for totals of 298, and so it was left with Jurado needing a 75 to win. As he neared home he began to falter – not badly, but he was taking fives when fours were required. Finally he arrived at the 18th green, a par five where the treacherous Barry Burn has to be crossed three times, requiring a birdie four to tie. After a perfect drive he elected to lay up short of the burn which crosses in front of the green. A good pitch followed, but it was never close enough to hope for a birdie. Just after holing out for a par he was given the news (which he already should have known) that he had needed a four to tie. Had he known that, he would surely have gone for the green, but who is to say what would have happened?

So, for a third time, following Lytham in 1926 and Sandwich in 1928, Jurado had missed out on taking the title. What a coup it would have been for Argentine golf had he done so. Remarkably, however, two of his fellow countrymen also finished in the top 11 places.

Tommy Armour's life story was an extraordinary one. Born in Edinburgh in 1896, he moved to the United States, having accompanied the Walker Cup side in 1922. He was blinded by mustard gas in the Great War, and his impaired eyesight led to his being an infamously slow player who took an age to line up his shots. Sarazen is quoted as saying of Armour that as an amateur he was only a 'fair' player but after turning professional in 1924 he became a great one. Not only a great player but a colourful one who became known as 'The Silver Scot'.

In addition to winning at Carnoustie, Armour won the US Open in 1927 and the US PGA in 1930, defeating Sarazen by one hole. He also became one of the most renowned teachers the game has known.

PERCY ALLISS

A LEADING BRITISH PROFESSIONAL *between the wars, Alliss was for many years attached to a club in Berlin and won the German Open five times. On nine occasions he finished in the top ten in the Open, his best year being 1931 when he was just two strokes behind Tommy Armour at Carnoustie.*

PETER ALLISS

P ETER ALLISS *was born into the game and like his father became a leading professional. A regular competitor in the Open, he finished in the top ten on five occasions. He won several events throughout Europe and played in eight Ryder Cup teams. For many years he has been part of the BBC golf commentary team and has also had a successful career as a golf course architect.*

1932 *Sarazen the King of Princes*

I̶N 1932 THE CHAMPIONSHIP moved to the Princes Golf Club, adjacent to Royal St George's for one occasion only *(see page 210 for further details of the Princes Golf Club)*.

When Walter Hagen and Gene Sarazen sailed to England to compete in the 1928 Open, Sarazen confided to Hagen one evening over cocktails that, having already won the US Open and two US PGA titles, the one thing he wanted more than anything else was the British Open. Hagen, with two Open titles already under his belt and possibly one or two dry martinis, replied that in order to achieve his ambition, Sarazen would need the best caddie available. Hagen then told Sarazen he could borrow his caddie, 'Skip' Daniels who he claimed to be the best.

Despite Sarazen taking up his offer, Hagen still won the 1928 title by two strokes with Sarazen blaming himself for ignoring Daniel's advice at the Canal Hole, resulting in a seven. Four years later Sarazen was advised that Daniels was no longer fit enough for the job and reluctantly gave him the bad news. Sarazen and his new caddie did not get on and his game deteriorated during a week of practice. With the championship just two days away, Lord Innis-Kerr visited Sarazen and gave him the news that Daniels was heartbroken at being dropped and suggested he re-employ him. Sarazen relented and gave Daniels one more chance.

The rest is history. Sarazen's game improved at once and he led the championship from start to finish, finishing five strokes clear of MacDonald Smith and six ahead of Arthur Havers.

Sarazen even asked for Daniels to be by his side for the presentation ceremony, a request that was sadly refused. Within months, Daniels was dead.

'When old Dan died the world was the poorer by one champion,' lamented Sarazen on hearing the news.

RIGHT: *Gene Sarazen plays to the 6th green at Princes, watched by his faithful caddie Skip Daniels. Sadly just months after their victory, Daniels died.*

Shute Makes It Ten in a Row for the USA

1933

~

1933 WAS ALSO A RYDER CUP YEAR and a mere two weeks after tasting the narrowest of defeats at Southport and Ainsdale the Americans repaired to St Andrews for the Open Championship. Back in Britain however, there was great hope, following the home success at Southport, of a much needed and long-awaited British victory.

At the end of the week, however, five of the top six finishers were Americans. On 292 were Densmore 'Denny' Shute, who had four 73s, and his fellow American Craig Wood. On 293 were Leo Diegel, Sarazen and Syd Easterbrook from the Knowle Park club in Kent. Disaster had befallen the latter two, Sarazen taking six on the devilishly difficult 11th (a steward had incorrectly 'accused' him of taking seven) and Easterbrook took a seven on the 14th.

An even worse event happened to Diegel. At the 72nd hole he laid a long approach putt close to the hole. Had it gone in he would have been Open champion, but he still had one more putt to tie. However, he failed completely to hit the ball! Was it nerves? Who knows what caused it, but a disappointed Diegel blamed no one but himself.

Henry Cotton, who for many years had been finishing in the top ten, was joint leader with one round to go but sadly fell away with a final 79. For him, however, glory lay just around the corner.

The following day Shute and Wood played 36 holes to decide the championship, with Shute winning an uneventful match by five strokes, 149 to 154. Joy at last for Shute, who at the Ryder Cup had three-putted on the final green in the deciding match against Easterbrook.

Born in Ohio but from a family originally hailing from Devon, Shute was a slightly built man with a compact swing and enormous powers of concentration. He went on to further sucess winning the USPGA in 1936 and 1937 when the game was still a matchplay event. Strangely he never really challenged seriously for the Open again although he had a fine record in the US Open.

Wood's career continued for many years and he had the dubious distinction of being runner-up in all four Major events, but he did win both the US Open and the Masters once apiece as well.

So, with huge British disappointment, the Open went to America for the tenth successive year, but this was to be the end of their golden era and the Championship title would not cross the Atlantic again until after the Second World War.

ABOVE: *Denny Shute played in few Open Championships but four 73s in 1933 were sufficient to tie with fellow American player Craig Wood. Victory was his following a 36-hole play-off.*

GOLF ILLUSTRATED
THE ONLY WEEKLY GOLF JOURNAL IN THE WORLD—Established in 1890.

No. 1898. Vol. CXXXIV (Copyright).   AUGUST 13th, 1938   (This newspaper is registered at the G.P.O.)   Price SIXPENCE

COTTON LEADS
THE BRITISH COMEBACK
1934-1939

AFTER TEN YEARS OF AMERICAN DOMINANCE, the British finally had a home winner to shout about, with Henry Cotton's victory at Sandwich. His win, his overall contribution to the game and his efforts to improve the image of the golf professional led to a British revival in the Championship, and five successive home victories followed.

It has to be said that in this period the challenge from the United States was not quite what it had been. Prize money in the States far exceeded what was on offer at the Open, and few players chose to make the long journey across the Atlantic that would result in missing two tournaments at home.

However, Cotton's victory at Carnoustie was achieved with the entire US Ryder Cup team in the field and no one can take that away from him. Although he won again, at Muirfield in 1948, there is no doubt that he was at his peak when war broke out, which probably robbed him of further victories.

RIGHT: *Henry Cotton in action at Royal St George's in 1934.*

LEFT: *The front cover of* Golf Illustrated *from August 1938 showing the dominance of the Dunlop golf ball.*

1934

A New Hero Is Born

W<small>HEN THE CHAMPIONSHIP RETURNED</small> to Royal St George's, the fact that there were only four Americans in the field was soon made academic when Henry Cotton produced rounds of 67 and 65 (he also did 66 in qualifying). His second round was a championship record which would last for 43 years, and to mark this achievement Dunlop named their rubber-core ball the 'Dunlop 65'.

Alf Padgham, following scores of 71 and 70, was in second position, but nine strokes behind Cotton!

The third and final day was blustery with squalls of rain and in the morning Cotton kept in control with a fine 72 under the conditions.

Australian-born Joe Kirkwood made up some ground with a 71, as did Syd Brews, an English-born South African, following his 70, but incredibly Cotton went into the final round with a ten-stroke lead!

BELOW: *Cotton chips from the back of 'The Maiden', the par three 6th at Sandwich.*

When he reappeared after lunch, however, he looked anything but the conquering hero. The story goes that he ate something disagreeable at lunch and was suffering from stomach cramps when he started out in the afternoon. Stroke

after stroke went and Cotton, out in 40, started back with three fives. Suddenly the outcome was uncertain and there was the possibility of the biggest 'blow up' in the history of the championship.

But he regrouped and put together three fours to stem the flow. The winning margin was eventually five strokes, Brews taking second place following a 71.

Cotton's record-equalling 283 was a great triumph for him, but even better was to follow in future years!

He was now hailed as the finest British golfer since the Great Triumvirate, who, incidentally, had all been present at Sandwich during the week. In his victory speech Cotton publicly thanked Braid and Taylor for their support, and before leaving Sandwich he visited Vardon, who on the final day had been confined to his bed at the Guildford Hotel. Cotton handed him the silver Claret Jug and both men wept openly.

ABOVE: *Henry Cotton at Royal St George's. His 36 and 54 hole scores smashed all existing records in any of the Majors and despite a last round 79, he was still champion by five strokes.*

1935

Fred Perry at Wimbledon . . .
. . . Alf Perry at Muirfield!

MUIRFIELD HOSTED its seventh championship in 1935 and Henry Cotton was a firm favourite to retain the title he had won the previous year at Sandwich. For 17 holes of the first round it looked likely that this would be the case, for Cotton stood on the 18th tee requiring a four for 66. But after a bunkered drive a six went down on the card – not that a 68 was exactly disastrous!

Next best was fellow Englishman Alf Perry, from the Leatherhead club in Surrey, one behind on 69. But Cotton's six did affect him somehow and he was not the same for the remainder of the week, mainly owing to a lack of confidence on the greens.

In the second round Perry returned a moderate 75 but this was followed by a 67 to equal Hagen's course record, sending him into the final 18 holes one ahead of Charles Whitcombe, the middle of the three well-known golfing brothers. However, Whitcombe ended with a disappointing 76 and was overhauled by one stroke by Alf Padgham, the professional from Sundridge Park.

So the championship depended on how Perry would stand up to the last-round pressure. A double bogey six on the very first hole, when just off the green in two, looked ominous, but he then played fearless golf, going for every shot and never holding back. The golfing gods were with him, and a 72 left him champion by four strokes from the other Alf – Padgham!

This was by far Perry's greatest success, and his only major win. He probably never received from the golfing public due credit for his game, but this victory at Muirfield was undoubtedly convincing and deserved. Perry also represented Great Britain and Ireland on three occasions in the Ryder Cup.

Note should be made of a name lower down the scoreboard in this championship, that of 22-year-old Welshman Dai Rees. This was the first year in a remarkable run which saw him finish in the top 30 in every Open until 1961.

ABOVE: *Open Champion Alf Perry proudly holding the Claret Jug after securing his two stroke victory at Muirfield.*

RIGHT: *Huge crowds watch as Alf Perry strides towards the 13th green in his last round at Muirfield in the 1935 Open Championship.*

Padgham Completes a British Hat-Trick

1936

BELOW: *Justice was done for Alf Padgham in 1936, following years of near success.*

OGDEN'S CIGARETTES

A. H. PADGHAM

WHEN THE CHAMPIONSHIP returned to Hoylake on the Lancashire coast in 1936 it naturally included all the top home players but only a handful of Americans challenged, led by Gene Sarazen.

The man in form, however, was Alf Padgham, who had followed his third place at Sandwich in 1934 and second place at Muirfield in 1935 by winning several events prior to Hoylake. With an effortless swing he made the game look extraordinarily easy. He was one of the longest hitters of his day, despite having a short backswing.

However, in 1936 it was his putter that won everything for him. He held it quite a distance from his body like an extension of his arms, rolled the ball smoothly towards the hole, and invariably in 1936 it disappeared into the cup!

When the final round began, Jimmy Adams, a fine player originally from Troon, led the championship with Henry Cotton, just a single stroke ahead of Padgham. The first to stumble, surprisingly, was Cotton, whose 74 left him with a four-round total of 289. Adams took 38 to the turn, but two long putts put him back in the picture. Needing a four at the 17th he was bunkered and a five resulted, and at the 18th a valiant putt for a three jumped in and out of the hole! Back in 35 for a 73 and Adams finished on 288, one ahead of Cotton.

And so it was all down to Padgham, who stood on the 18th tee needing a four to tie and three to win. A fine drive, an easy-looking pitch to 12 feet and down went the putt for victory! Alf Padgham was the quietest and most modest of Open Champions, but what a way to win! 1936 was certainly his year of glory.

Padgham's family had close ties with the delightful Royal Ashdown Forest Club in Sussex, where he served his apprenticeship, but for many years at the height of his career he represented the Sundridge Park club near Sevenoaks in Kent.

JIMMY ADAMS

BORN IN TROON in 1910, Adams was one of the leading British professionals before and after the Second World War. He twice finished second in the Open, in 1936 and in 1938. In 1951 he led after a first-round 68, only to finish fourth, and in 1954 he was fifth to Peter Thomson at Birkdale. A member of four Ryder Cup teams, Adams was a loyal supporter of the Open over 25 years.

1937

Cotton's Finest Hour

A CARNOUSTIE COURSE at its full length, well over 7,000 yards, with extra bunkers strategically placed in the fairways, was the challenge that met the competitors for the 1937 Open. These included the entire US Ryder Cup team, recently victorious at Southport – among them some new but soon to be famous names such as Byron Nelson and Sam Snead. But after two rounds it was Reg, the youngest of the Whitcombe brothers, who led, stung perhaps by his exclusion from the Ryder Cup team.

The third and final day produced horrendous weather and it is said that every shop in Carnoustie sold out of waterproofs – nothing would keep the resolute Scots from watching!

Despite a 74 in the morning (not a bad score in the conditions) Reg Whitcombe, on 216, still led, followed on 218 by his brother Charles and Byron Nelson. A stroke behind was Henry Cotton, with fellow Englishman Charles Lacey (brother of the professional Arthur Lacey) a further two behind him.

Lacey's fine last round of 72 was to leave him in third position on 293, but neither Charles Whitcombe nor Nelson could make an impression, finishing with 76 and 74 respectively. Reg Whitcombe finished with a 76 to take second place on 292, no mean achievement, but for him there were greater things on the horizon.

Some distance behind on the course was Cotton, and he knew exactly what was required to win. In the torrential downpour he chipped and putted his way round, taking just 26 putts and never taking more than a five. His 71, still regarded by some as one of the greatest rounds ever carded to win a major championship, left him on 290 and two strokes ahead of the field.

This second Open win undoubtedly gave Cotton the recognition he so greatly craved, and although he won a third title 11 years later at Muirfield this period of his career was considered to be his finest.

By now he had left the Waterloo Club in Belgium and in January 1937 he joined the Ashridge Club near Berkhampstead. It was here, on the spur of the Chiltern Hills, that Cotton built his house, 'Shangri-La', named after the valley in James Hilton's book *The Lost Horizon*.

With the 1937 championship approaching, Cotton visited Carnoustie in May. He hadn't played there before but he reported it to be in poor condition. This is another example of how much the event has changed. As a public links the course would have stayed open until only a week or so prior to the championship and only then been tidied up somewhat. Imagine that sort of preparation today!

ABOVE: *Henry Cotton's last round 71 at Carnoustie in 1937, played in torrential rain is still considered one of the great 'Open' rounds.*

Whitcombe Weathers the Storm   1938

THE CHAMPIONSHIP RETURNED to Sandwich in 1938, the scene of Walter Hagen's two victories and Henry Cotton's first just four years previously. The event had been scheduled for Deal, but storm damage and flooding had necessitated a switch to nearby Royal St George's.

As it was not a Ryder Cup year there was a dearth of Americans.

The most memorable thing about this championship was the weather and its variation. The first two days were calm, the sun shone and the larks sang. With three players (Dick Burton, Jack Busson and Bill Cox) tied on 140, a record score seemed imminent. Just behind came Jimmy Adams, Reg Whitcombe, Alf Padgham and Henry Cotton. Overnight, however, there was a violent gale and the picture changed completely.

On arrival at the course the following day the sight greeting everyone was horrifying. The huge eight-masted exhibition tent, the largest ever at the championship, had been torn to shreds. Twisted metal lay everywhere, assorted goods on sale at the exhibition were strewn over the course and as far as Princes. This was to be one of the worst days' weather in Open history.

After rounds of 70 and 71 Adams took two 78s, Padgham took 82 and the three overnight leaders fell away with scores into the 80s. Cotton's 77 in the morning was a respectable score but his afternoon 74 was a remarkable one. Out in 35 and starting home 4,3,3, victory seemed his, but 29 strokes for the last six holes was his undoing. His 151 for the last two rounds was the lowest of the day. However, the title went to Whitcombe, who followed his morning 75 with a more than respectable 78 in the conditions.

His triumph was thoroughly deserved. The final day had been a day for giants, and Whitcombe had played like one.

RIGHT: *A scene of devastation greeted players and spectators alike on the final morning of the 1938 championship. The Exhibition Tent was torn to shreds by the overnight storm.*

1939 — *Burton Wins with War Looming*

SOME NEW FACES APPEARED on the scene when what turned out to be the last championship before the war was played at St Andrews in 1939. From the United States came Johnny Bulla of Chicago, who would challenge many times, and Lawson Little, who as an amateur had the unique record of winning the Amateur Championships of Britain and America in the same year, not once but twice! That was in 1934 and 1935, and by now he had turned professional. From Argentina came Martin Pose, who had just won the French Open, and from South Africa Bobby Locke, of whom we were to hear much more after the war.

Little's play in the qualifying rounds was encouraging, but in the event itself he disappointed. Pose played well, but an eight at the Road Hole, including a two-stroke penalty for grounding his club on the grass beside the road, which was technically part of the hazard, ruined his chances. Bobby Locke had a fine first-round 70, astonishing in that it included an eight at the 14th! Dick Burton and

BELOW: *Dick Burton holes the winning putt in the 1939 Open. At the peak of his career, who knows what Burton may have achieved but for the outbreak of war.*

Jack Busson, who had shared a distant fourth position at Sandwich the previous year also started well with 70s.

As the players started the final round the lead lay with a relatively unknown player, Johnny Fallon of Huddersfield, with a total of 215, but sadly a 79 ruined his hopes of glory. Bill Shankland, a rugged player who had once played professional rugby in Australia, lay second on 217, but a 77 destroyed his chances. Alf Perry, champion in 1935, came next on 218, but he too fell away with a closing 76.

The destiny of the title lay in the hands of Bulla, whose rounds of 77, 71 and 71 left him well placed, and Burton, who had represented Great Britain and Ireland in the two previous Ryder Cups and was a regular on the tournament scene. Bulla finished with a 73 that left Burton, who was out late, requiring a 72 to win.

Out in 35, he sailed through the treacherous 14th and all but secured victory on the next two holes. An eight-footer disappeared on the 15th, and at the 16th after four poor shots his putt fell in for a five and he was almost home. A sensible five at the Road Hole left him in the classic position of needing a four to win the Open!

A colossal drive over the road at the final hole left him a short pitch that he nonchalantly flicked to within five or six yards of the pin. With two putts for victory the first seemed to be going a good yard past. Burton strode after it and as he did so the ball dropped into the hole! So victory was his, and with it a sixth consecutive British success!

Dick Burton continued to be prominent in golf for many years, and in Brighton in 1942 he won a tournament with rounds of 68, 66, 64 and 68, his aggregate of 266 then being a record low total for a major British 72-hole event. In latter life he was for many years the professional at Coombe Hill in Surrey.

The championship had come a long way, but the clouds of war were looming.

ABOVE: *Johnny Bulla, one of very few Americans to support the Open in the late 1930s and just after the war. He finished in second place in the 1939 and 1946 Championships at St Andrews.*

THE ERA OF LOCKE AND THOMSON

1946-1959

With the exception of Sam Snead's victory at St Andrews in 1946 and Ben Hogan's, on his only appearance in the Open, at Carnoustie in 1953, the Americans tended to stay at home chasing dollars rather than Open titles. There were, however, overseas challenges from elsewhere.

Arthur D'Arcy Locke, known as 'Bobby', was born in Germiston, South Africa, in November 1917 and at the age of 16 was a scratch golfer. His record as a young player was quite remarkable. Aged 18, he won the 1935 South African Open itself, the first of nine times he would do so.

In 1936, the mining company he worked for sent him to London, and the same year he finished in eighth place at Hoylake in the Open, as an amateur and still only 19 years old.

Following the war Locke won 13 events in the United States in a short space of time and won his first Open Championship at Sandwich in 1949. He is one of only a few players who have successfully defended their title, which he did at Troon in 1950 with a then record-breaking score of 279, and he won again in 1952 at Royal Lytham.

By the time of Locke's fourth and final victory, at St Andrews in 1957, a young Australian, Peter Thomson, had begun an even more remarkable sequence by winning a hat-trick of victories in 1954, 1955 and 1956. Thomson would add a further two victories to become one of a very select group of players (there are now five in all) who have won five times or more. He was also runner-up on three occasions, and his record from 1952 to 1958 is quite remarkable – 2, 2, 1, 1, 1, 2, 1.

In the late 1950s, another young overseas star arrived on the scene: Gary Player, from South Africa, who would become one of the championship's most dominant figures for a further two decades.

LEFT: *Bobby Locke arrives in London in 1953 on his way to Carnoustie.*

RIGHT: *The 17th Road Hole in St Andrews in the 1940s. With a road to the right of the narrowest of greens and a cavernous bunker to the left, countless rounds have been ruined here.*

1946

Snead Steals the Show

~

ABOVE: *Sam Snead demonstrating one of the most fluent swings the game has ever seen. He claimed both the Masters and US PGA titles on three occasions.*

WITH THE WORLD STILL TRYING to get back on its feet after the ravages of six years of war, 1946 saw the championship return to St Andrews. Understandably there were few new young players to challenge or take over from the pre-war leaders of the game.

Although still prestigious, the Open had lost some of its lustre as the US circuit had developed. For the American professional golfer it was far more lucrative to pick up a regular cheque on that side of the Atlantic than to struggle over to Britain, miss two events at home and suffer from the time change.

However, overseas players did come to St Andrews and they included Bobby Locke, from South Africa, and Norman von Nida, a young Australian professional who was to spend much time in the UK in years to come. The Americans Lawson Little and Johnny Bulla both returned, having played in the 1939 Open at St Andrews, and so too did Sam Snead, who had played once before at Carnoustie in 1937. Snead had made his mind up to play at the last minute and arrived only two days before the championship started, encouraged, it is rumoured, by a putting lesson from Walter Hagen.

In 1939 Henry Cotton had made suggestions about crowd control and this year drastic steps were taken to provide for the players and spectators alike. The spectators were entirely excluded from the playing area, with barriers and crossing places installed. It could be argued that it made for improved watching as the crowd was better spread.

After two days all the big names were at the top of the leader board. Cotton led after two 70s, followed by Snead on 141. On 142 was Dai Rees of Wales, who would go on to have a marvellous Open record. His second round was 67, a remarkable score at the time. One stroke back were Bulla and Locke, who had had a 69 on the first day. The Road Hole, the 17th, has ruined many a card over the decades, and this happened on the first day to Bulla when he only needed a 4, 4 finish for a fine score of 68. His second found the road which, it must be remembered, was not the tarmac and relatively level surface that it is today. He failed to get off the first time, his fourth ran over the green into the notorious bunker, he exploded out, and two putts later a seven went down on the card. With a four at the last he was round in 71 – no mean score, but at the end of the week he must have rued that hole.

The final day produced more wind, with the lowest score in the morning among the leaders being Bulla's 72. This left a three-way tie on 215, as the afternoon round got under way, involving Snead, Bulla and Rees. For Rees, playing into a strong headwind, one hole was enough effectively to end his challenge. A visit to the Swilcan Burn resulted in a nightmare seven from which he never recovered, his round ending in 80.

1946

Locke, who had started three behind, made a great three at the 1st and was back in contention. Out in 36 and one under fours after 12 holes, it seemed that for the first time a South African name would be inscribed on the Claret Jug. But for no apparent reason his putting fell apart and with three putts on the 15th, 16th and 18th holes he finished in 76. When he three putted on the 15th it was the first time he had done so in the championship, a remarkable performance when one considers the size of the greens at St Andrews.

Cotton, only one stroke off the lead at lunch, having put his second to the 1st in the Swilcan Burn, started with five consecutive fives and his chance was gone. He was to finish in 79, his 155 strokes for the day being 15 more than he had taken over the previous two rounds. To be fair to Cotton he was recovering from a major operation and had hardly played for a year.

Bulla too was disappointed. Following a six at the Road Hole he required just a four at the last to overtake Locke. His first putt went just 18 inches past the hole, but incredibly he missed the one back.

So it was left to Snead, who of those with a chance of winning was last out. Having driven well in the wind throughout the first two days, he sliced his drive almost out of bounds on the opening hole and a five went down on the card. He was lucky at the 5th, when he crashed a brassie way into the whins but found his ball and somehow made a five. From there it was plain sailing and with a birdie at the long 14th the pressure was off. In the end his margin of victory was four strokes, but how different it might have been had the gods not been smiling on him at the 5th.

Snead was never to challenge in the latter stages of an Open again, but he did have an extraordinary career in the United States, with three Masters and three US PGA victories. Strangely he never won the US Open, although he was runner-up on four occasions. After eight Ryder Cup appearances (captain on three occasions) he was still playing fine golf and as late as 1974, aged 62, finished joint third in the US PGA!

His swing will be remembered as one of the most fluent, rhythmic and classical of all time, and even now, in his eighties, he still strikes the ball well.

JOHNNY FALLON

*B*ORN IN LANARK IN SCOTLAND *in 1913, Fallon was a regular competitor in the Open for more than 20 years. In 1939 at St Andrews he held a two stroke lead entering the final round but a disastrous 79 saw him finish fourth, four strokes behind Dick Burton. Sixteen years later, in 1955, having done nothing in the championship for some time, he showed his liking for St Andrews again, by finishing second, just two stokes behind Peter Thomson.*

1947

Daly Crosses the Water for Open Success

H OYLAKE HOSTED THE CHAMPIONSHIP in early July and the crowds were treated to one of the most exciting finishes ever, with no one daring to name the winner right up to the last minute.

Only three Americans travelled over to challenge: Vic Ghezzi, a fine player on the US circuit, Johnny Bulla once again, and Frank Stranahan, an ambitious amateur who would feature strongly in this championship and again in 1953.

BELOW: *Fred Daly cheered by fans after his Open triumph. He followed this by winning the British Matchplay title in the same year.*

Henry Cotton, the favourite, started well with a 69 but a second-round 78 lost him some ground.

With one round to play, four players shared the lead on 221: Fred Daly from Belfast, Norman von Nida from Australia, Cotton and Arthur Lees (later professional at Sunningdale for many years), with several others snapping close at their heels.

Early in the last round another player suddenly came into the picture. Reg Horne, the professional at Hendon, finished with a 71, having crept up the leader board in the morning with a 72. After starting with two modest rounds of 77 and 74 he suddenly found himself sitting in the clubhouse as leader, and possibly the next Open Champion!

Out half an hour or so after Horne was Daly, and after an unexciting first nine of 38 he started home 3, 3, 4, 3, 4, 4, 4! However, a six at the 17th was a setback, leaving him requiring a four at the last to tie Horne. Two fine strokes to the 408-yard closing hole left him some 12 yards from the hole, and incredibly the putt went in to give Daly the lead on 293.

The other joint leaders going into the last round – von Nida, Cotton and Lees – took 76 to spoil their chances, so now the only player capable of catching Daly was the American amateur Stranahan. A fine birdie four at the 16th left him requiring to play the final two holes, both par fours, in seven strokes to tie. Safely on in two at the 17th he boldly went for the putt, only to miss the one back. Now he needed a two at the last, and the crowd of thousands gasped as his six-iron approach landed short, rolled up to the pin, and stopped a mere two inches short of the hole!

So Daly was victorious by a single stroke and a worthy champion at that. Not the most stylish of golfers, his wide arc and consequent movement away from the ball gave his swing the appearance of a lurch. But for a small man he commanded great length and for a while reigned supreme. Victory in the Irish Open, three British Matchplay Championship wins and four Ryder Cup appearances were the other highlights of an illustrious career.

Daly was one of Gene Sarazen's playing partners at Troon in 1973 when Sarazen had his historic hole in one at the Postage Stamp.

1947

ABOVE: *Stranahan's success in the 1940s to the 1950s was exceptional.*

CHARLIE WARD

BORN IN BIRMINGHAM in 1911, Ward was based as a professional at Torquay and for 25 years was a regular Open competitor. His record from 1946 to 1951 was superb – fourth in 1946, sixth in 1947, third in 1948, fourth in 1949 and third in 1951. A small wiry figure with a lightning fast swing, he had a wonderful short game gained from endless hours of practice. As well as a fine Open record he also won the Dunlop Masters in 1949, his finest year, when he also won three other events and the Vardon trophy for the lowest stroke average throughout the season.

1948

Cotton Confounds the Critics

ABOVE: *Cotton celebrates his third Open success, at Muirfield in 1948. His second round 66 was the foundation of his five stroke victory.*

AFTER TWO ROUNDS of the 1948 Open at Muirfield it looked certain that Henry Cotton was on his way to a third triumph in the championship. An opening 71 followed by a record 66, watched all the way by George VI, gave him a six-stroke lead over Fred Daly, Alf Padgham, Norman von Nida, Charlie Ward of England and a newcomer from Argentina, Roberto de Vicenzo.

Cotton was desperate for victory following murmurings that perhaps his game was not quite what it used to be. He had practised hard for Muirfield and arrived at the peak of his game, confident about his chances and really only fearing de Vicenzo, a magnificent player on his first visit to the British Isles, but surely not aided by being unable to speak a word of English.

A first round of 71 left Cotton well placed, but it was his second-round 66 that helped him to take control of the championship. Two almost perfect nines of 33 gave him the course record that had stood at 67 since Walter Hagen's 67 in 1929!

There were a number of critical moments in Cotton's third round, played with the wind blowing from the north-west and making conditions distinctly testing. Out in 39 and with two fives starting for home, his overnight lead was rapidly disappearing. But with great determination and aided with a three at the 12th and a two at the 13th he finished with a 75. On 212 he led at lunchtime by a two from Alf Padgham, and by three strokes from Sam King, de Vicenzo, Dai Rees and Flory van Donck of Belgium, who in years to come built up a remarkable Open record, finishing in the top ten nine years out of 11, and twice being beaten only by the winner. Aided by a third round hole in one on the 13th Charlie Ward was just four strokes behind.

Despite a shanked bunker shot on the 18th, resulting in a dropped shot, Cotton gave his opponents little chance. His last round of 72 left him four strokes ahead of Fred Daly who put up a most spirited defence of his title.

Cotton's third Open triumph was his last, and his contribution to the game over so many decades cannot be overestimated. He will be remembered as much for his playing record as for striving to improve the standing of the golf professional. At the end of his career he became involved in golf course architecture – Penina in Portugal was one of his more notable designs, and became his home as well.

In 1987, very belatedly, Cotton was awarded a knighthood, but sadly died before the honour could officially be bestowed on him.

Locke and Bradshaw 'Bottle' It Out 1949

THE OPEN CHAMPIONSHIP of 1949 was a truly memorable one. The event was scheduled to be played at Deal, but the course had not recovered sufficiently from wartime requisitioning, and just as in 1938 the championship moved a short way along the coast to Royal St George's.

It saw the return of Bobby Locke, the famous South African player who had won the championship of his own country at the age of 17 and had come so close in two Open Championships at St Andrews in 1939 and 1946. He had made a huge impact in the United States, winning six events and coming second in two others in his first season there in 1947.

In the first round Locke played beautifully for 13 holes and stood on the 14th tee six under fours. Then a sliced drive out of bounds led to a seven and ultimately a 69, but a second-round 76 did not help his cause.

The first two days saw excellent golf from Charlie Ward, Roberto de Vicenzo and Max Faulkner, but they all trailed local Kent man Sam King, the professional from Knole Park, who was on 140.

Out early on the last day was the Irishman from Kilcroney, Harry Bradshaw, a regular on the British circuit, and a fine 68 leapt him into contention. Locke was out half an hour later and despite a dropped stroke at the

RIGHT: *In glorious weather, Bobby Locke drives from the 18th tee while practising for the 1949 championship.*

1949

RIGHT: *Bobby Locke and Harry Bradshaw together following their 36-hole play-off. Locke's superb two round total 135 gave him victory by twelve strokes.*

15th he too completed a 68 that kept him level with Bradshaw. Max Faulkner's 71 meant that the three were tied entering the final round, with Locke, naturally, the favourite to win. Faulkner did fade, and ended in 74, but Bradshaw's game held together and, aided by a little luck when his second jumped the Canal after a topped shot, he was round in 70 for a total of 283.

Out in 32, Locke looked to have the championship in the bag, but suddenly his game changed. A stroke went at the 10th after three putts, and the cross-bunker at the 15th cost him another. Having led comfortably he now needed three pars to tie with Bradshaw. He dropped a shot immediately at the short 16th, but this was remedied with an immaculate three at the 17th. The 17th at Sandwich is never the easiest hole at which to make a birdie, let alone in the Open Championship when under such severe pressure. Two strokes to the edge of the final green, a delicate chip to three feet and a putt left Locke matching Bradshaw's 70 and 283.

The following day the two played off over 36 holes, but Bradshaw had had his chance. Two rounds totalling 147 was no disgrace, but Locke was irresistible and his astonishing total of 135 gave him victory by 12 strokes and his first Open triumph. In 36 holes he was worse than four just once when he took five at the 15th in the afternoon round.

This championship will always be remembered for an incident involving Bradshaw at the 5th in the second round when his ball lodged in a broken beer bottle! Rather than wait for a ruling to see if he was entitled to relief (which at the time he was not, but would be now) he played the ball as it lay. With his eyes closed he hit at the ball but only moved it some 20 yards, and a six was the result. No one can say for certain that this incident at such an early stage affected the outcome of the championship, but on his own admission it took him six holes to regain his composure, and a 77 was the end product.

He had much consolation, however, winning ten Irish Professional Championships, two Irish Opens, the Dunlop Masters twice, making three Ryder Cup appearances and in 1958 with Christy O'Connor winning the Canada Cup for Ireland in Mexico City.

For the record Locke's financial reward for his Open victory was £300, double that of the first prize just three years before.

Locke Champion Again

~

1950

After a gap of 27 years the championship returned to Troon on the Ayrshire coast of Scotland. Old Troon, as it is known, had been considered perhaps too dependent on the prevailing winds from the west to be in the front rank of championship courses.

The wind blew during practice but dropped completely for the championship, resulting in a winning total of 279, four strokes lower than the previous record. Understandably Locke started the championship a red-hot favourite. With the fairways baked hard and running fast he used just a brassie or spoon off the tee and, incredibly, in 72 holes missed the fairway just twice! The greens were watered every evening and were in excellent condition, like 'velvet' as they were described. As one of the greatest putters of all time, such perfect greens to play upon would have done Locke's chances no harm.

The leader board after two rounds was full of familiar names. Dai Rees led on 139, with Locke, de Vicenzo and Max Faulkner all within striking distance. Locke's second-round 72 was a fine effort as it included a six on the short 5th, where he fluffed a chip shot into a bunker. However, he fought back bravely with four birdies in the next six holes.

On the third and final day Fred Daly, champion three years before at Hoylake suddenly came on the scene with two superb rounds of 69 and 66 for a total of 282. Rees, with rounds of 72 and 71 matched Daly's 282, leaving Locke and de Vicenzo to battle it out for the title.

De Vicenzo, not playing at his best but putting like a demon, finished with a 70 for 281 to lead by one. Locke was out just behind, knowing exactly what he had to do. He played immaculate golf, his only error being a missed putt from four feet on the 12th. Following a fine pitch and putt for par at the difficult 17th he stood on the final tee with the luxury of needing just a five to take the title. A solid par four was achieved and Locke had secured his second consecutive Open victory with a record breaking total.

The Great Triumvirate had all won successive championships, as had Jones and Hagen, and of the current generation there was no one more worthy to join that distinguished company than Locke.

The score of the German amateur Herman Tissies on the Postage Stamp 8th was far less distinguished. Having missed the green with his tee shot he then proceeded to go from one bunker to another, eventually single putting for a 15.

Below: *Bobby Locke, whose four round total 279 at Troon in 1950 set a new Open Championship record.*

1951   *Flamboyant Faulkner Wins at Portrush*

For the first and as yet the only time the championship was held off mainland Britain, at Royal Portrush, a wonderful links course on the Antrim coast at the top of Northern Ireland. With its breathtaking views, Portrush is without doubt one of the truly great links. The fairways are narrow, the rough really is rough, and the greens are both small and undulating!

In 1951 the choice of Portrush was popular with the players, but lack of accessibility resulted in smaller crowds than had been anticipated. The fact that the championship has not returned there is not a reflection on the quality of the course itself.

For the first time the BBC gave full coverage to an Open, with commentators scattered around the course giving up-to-the-minute coverage to radio listeners.

Bobby Locke, champion in the previous two years, was the natural favourite but after two rounds it was Max Faulkner who led with scores of 71 and 70. Max Faulkner's ambition since the age of 12 had been to win the Open Championship. His father, Gus, was professional at Bexhill, Pennard in Wales and Bramley, and so Max learnt the game from an early age. By the time he was just 15 he was good enough to qualify for the 1932 Open at Princes. He spent time as assistant to Henry Cotton at Royal Mid Surrey before becoming the professional at St George's Hill.

By the time the championship went to Portrush, Faulkner had become a household name on the golf circuit, partly because of his flamboyance, that livened up tournaments considerably. With his liking for wearing shocking colours, often including canary yellow shoes, Faulkner caused quite a stir.

His form on arrival for the championship had not been good, but he had a fine record at Portrush, having twice come second in the Irish Open.

On the final morning, at the 16th, he played an extraordinary second shot. Up against an obstruction, and having to adopt a strange stance, he played an enormous slice that somehow bent back on to the green – whereupon his playing partner, the American amateur Frank Stranahan, came over to him and shook his hand, saying it was the finest shot he had ever seen!

His morning round of 70 left him with a six-stroke lead over the amicable Argentinian Antonio Cerda and the Englishman Norman Sutton. The rising star from Australia, Peter Thomson, was a further stroke back, with Harry Weetman and Locke too far back for a serious challenge, eight strokes off the lead. The title was Faulkner's for the taking.

It is at this stage that an apocryphal story should be laid to rest. Stories abound of Faulkner signing autographs the previous evening and adding after his name 'Open Champion 1951'. But Faulkner claims this is a total exaggeration and all that happened was, on approaching the 1st tee prior to the last round he bent down to tie up his laces, stood up and was asked for an autograph by a young boy who proffered a golf ball. It was duly signed and the boy's father then said, 'Excuse me, Mr Faulkner, could you add "Open Champion", because you are going to win, aren't you?' Having obliged, Faulkner thought to himself, 'My God, what have I done? I'd better not lose it now.' He claims it gave him even more determination for the afternoon!

1951

LEFT: *Eventual Open Champion Max Faulkner plays to the 72nd green at Royal Portrush watched by an eager crowd of spectators.*

Six strokes clear going into the final round, and then out in 37, Faulkner had the championship almost in his pocket.

Only Cerda, out in 34, appeared to have a chance of securing victory, but a six at the par-three 14th, the very aptly named 'Calamity Corner', totally wrecked his chances. With a safe five on the final hole Faulkner was round in 74 for a total of 285, and after a tense wait of three-quarters of an hour for player and spectators alike he was Open Champion by two strokes. It was really his favourite 11oz putter that had won him the championship, for in the four rounds his total putts were 27, 24, 29 and 29, and he never took more than a five.

The celebrations had to wait, for he flew straight back to Heathrow that evening and the following day was playing in a Fathers vs. Sons cricket match at his son's school!

His was a popular win, for not only had the Claret Jug returned to Britain, but both the style of Faulkner and his play were much to the crowd's liking. He could be compared with Hagen and Sarazen in his colourfulness and style.

Faulkner is the only person to have won the Open, the British Matchplay Championship (Ganton, 1953) and the Dunlop Masters (Wentworth, 1951). He also won the Spanish Open on three occasions and went on to much success in Senior events, winning the British Seniors Championship twice, at Aldeburgh in 1968 and Longniddry in 1970.

In 1973 Faulkner was one of Gene Sarazen's partners at Troon when the American recorded his famous hole in one at the Postage Stamp, 41 years after seeing him win the 1932 Championship!

His Open record was a remarkable one, for when he played at Carnoustie in 1975 for the final time it was 43 years after his first appearance. Faulkner was also a great supporter of charity work and played in excess of 250 exhibition matches for Cancer Relief.

Third Title for Locke

1952

FOR THE FIRST TIME since Bobby Jones's famous victory in 1926, the championship returned to the Royal Lytham and St Annes Golf Club.

The overseas challenge was led by Bobby Locke, Peter Thomson, Flory van Donck, Norman von Nida and Antonio Cerda, but with the exception of 50-year-old Gene Sarazen there was hardly an American to be found in the field.

Fred Daly, champion at nearby Hoylake five years earlier, led following superb rounds of 67 and 69, and despite a third-round 77 went into the final afternoon a stroke ahead of Locke and five ahead of Thomson, with the rest trailing in their wake.

Locke finished early on, and his 73 appeared good enough when Daly faltered with a six at the 15th. To his credit he fought back strongly but his 76 was not quite good enough, leaving him two strokes adrift of the South African.

But Thomson was still out on the course and the news filtered through that he was out in 36 and had then made a two at the short 12th. He gave it his all, but even with a four at the 17th and a birdie three at the last he just failed to catch Locke. In the end the difference was just a single stroke.

And so, emulating Harry Vardon and James Braid, Bobby Locke had won his third Open title in the space of four years.

LEFT: *Bobby Locke splashes out of a bunker to the 6th green at Royal Lytham St Annes in 1952. A last round 73 just held off the challenge of the pretender to his crown – Peter Thomson.*

RIGHT: *Twenty years after his Open success, Gene Sarazen was to finish a creditable 17th at the age of fifty.*

1953

Hogan Crowned King of the Links

CARNOUSTIE, ARGUABLY THE stiffest championship test in Britain, hosted its first Open since Cotton's triumph of 1937.

All attention was focused on the Texan, Ben Hogan, who miraculously had recovered from a near fatal car crash in 1949. His body had been shattered to such an extent that he had to learn to walk again. It is astonishing that he managed to return to play in the US Open in 1950, let alone win it. To do so he had to play two rounds on the final day and return the next to win in an 18-hole play-off with George Fazio and Lloyd Mangrum.

In 1953 Hogan had won the first two Major Championships of the year, the Masters and the US Open at Oakmont. On his first trip to Britain, and after a full week of practice using the small ball which he had never played before, he was a red-hot favourite.

Rain, hail, sunshine, Scottish mist and a brief but fierce wind were all present at some stage for the 91 competitors who had successfully qualified on the nearby Burnside course and the championship course itself. Exemption from qualifying did not exist, and the reigning Masters and US Open champion was treated like everybody else!

LEFT: *Ben Hogan on his way to a famous victory at Carnoustie. His record in the Majors between 1950 and 1953 included six victories in the nine events he entered.*

Fourth Title for Locke

1957

BOBBY LOCKE ARRIVED AT ST ANDREWS for the 1957 Open utterly determined to win. There were several reasons. One was that he did not like to lose! Another was his acute disappointment the previous year in missing the cut. The third reason was a young man called Gary Player, who was threatening to topple him as the reigning king of South African golf. Having already won three titles, Locke still felt he could emulate Taylor and Braid and perhaps even equal Harry Vardon's six wins.

Eric Brown made a good start, as in previous years, with four opening birdies courtesy of four putts each reputed to be in excess of 30 feet! His excellent 67 gave him a share of the lead after the first day with fellow Scot Laurie Ayton. Steady golf for the remainder of the championship left Brown with a total of 283 and a more than commendable third place.

Dick Smith, another Scot, and an amateur at that, would finish joint fifth on 286, a wonderful achievement. He went on to play in the 1959 Walker Cup side and had the rare distinction of winning the Amateur Championships of three different countries – Scotland, India and Portugal.

However, it was Locke and Thomson who were to battle it out for the championship despite both being in the Swilcan Burn in the second round. At the halfway stage Locke led by one and following a third-round 68 had a three-stroke cushion. As we all know, three strokes is not an insurmountable lead, but as the final round progressed it was clear that Thomson could not reduce the margin. Poor putting and a dropped stroke to par rather than an expected birdie at the par-five 5th did not help. Despite a wonderful run of five threes around The Loop at the far end of the course, Thomson just could not bridge the gap. At the 17th, needing a three, or a four at worst, he took five and Locke was champion for a fourth time, but not without a touch of drama at the end.

Some time after the presentation ceremony a protest was lodged claiming that on the last green he had marked his ball a couple of putter heads to the side to give his playing partner a clear line to the hole, but that when he replaced it he had not put it back on the correct spot. After much deliberating by the championship committee and viewing of the relevant newsreel it was decided that Locke had gained no advantage, he had won by three strokes anyway, and the result would stand. The instigator of the protest was never revealed. Was it a spectator, a rules fanatic, or could it have been one of Locke's closest challengers? We shall never know! What is certain is that it haunted Locke for a long, long time.

BELOW: *Bobby Locke celebrates his fourth and final victory at St Andrews in 1957, ending Peter Thomson's stranglehold on the event. His four round total of 279 gave him victory over Thomson by three strokes.*

1957

RIGHT: *Flory van Donck of Belgium had a superb Open record in the 1950s. He was fifth on three occasions and twice runner-up.*

1957 was Locke's final Open triumph. By now he had put on considerable weight, which did not help. In 1960 he was involved in a serious road accident on a level crossing, which affected his sight, and although he returned to play Seniors golf he was never quite the same player again.

Locke was a fierce competitor and something of a hero to the crowds, although a notoriously slow player. He played his shots with a pronounced draw and was one of the finest putters the game has ever seen.

This was the first year that the climax to the championship was shown live on television and also the first year that the leaders went out last for the third and fourth rounds.

ERIC BROWN

A FIERY SCOTSMAN, Brown was a regular in the Open for twenty years as well as a Ryder Cup player on four occasions and twice non-playing captain. Six times in the top ten, his finest years were 1957 and 1958 when finishing third behind Bobby Locke and Peter Thomson. Brown had a perfect singles record in Ryder Cup singles: played four, won four.

DAVID THOMAS

A FINE PLAYER from Wales, Thomas has the unenviable record of twice being runner up in the Open but the two men that defeated him were no less than Peter Thomson (only after a play-off) and Jack Nicklaus. Following a professional career that included four Ryder cup appearances, he became a leading golf course architect in partnership with Peter Alliss.

Thomson Back in Charge – Just 1958

ROYAL LYTHAM HOSTED the 1958 championship, and the spectators were delighted to find that the amenities had been greatly improved.

Former champions Gene Sarazen and Henry Cotton were in the field, as were Fred Daly, Bobby Locke and Max Faulkner. Locke was to finish tied for 16th, a good performance after a disappointing opening round of 76.

Eric Brown put up another fine performance to finish in third place for the second consecutive year, but the destiny of the title ultimately lay between three times champion Peter Thomson and Dave Thomas of Wales, who had finished in fifth place the previous year.

Thomson had staked his claim for the championship with rounds of 66 and 72 (in qualifying he recorded a 63), but at the halfway stage Irishman Christy O'Connor led following a 67 and a 68. A 73 followed, and so the main challenge

BELOW: *Watched intently, Peter Thomson plays to the 14th green in his 1958 play-off victory over Wales's Dave Thomas. The pair had tied on a record low score of 278.*

1958

to Thomson (third round 67) and Thomas (69) came from him, Brown with an extraordinary third round of 65, Argentinian Leopoldo Ruiz (who had had a second-round 65) and van Donck, who had a third round 67.

In the final round van Donck never got going and finished with a 74, but Ruiz had a great opportunity at least to tie for the championship until a disastrous seven on the final hole ruined his chances. O'Connor, playing with Ruiz, also had a great chance, but a bunkered tee shot at the last cost him a crucial stroke. Brown continued to attack, and when he stood on the 18th tee it seemed a four would be good enough for victory. But he too was bunkered off the tee, a tragic and ultimately crucial six followed, and his total of 279 was one too many.

Thomson and Thomas were paired together and after 17 holes they stood on the final tee level. Thomas's second ended some 15 yards from the pin, and his brave putt for a birdie ended just 18 inches past the hole. This left Thomson with a putt of some 12 feet for outright victory, but his putt never looked like dropping, and so a play-off the following day was required.

An immense crowd had seen a pulsating last day but the play-off, alas, as so often, was something of an anticlimax, although to his credit Thomas stuck to Thomson for one and a half of the two rounds. The final scores were Thomson 139, Thomas 143.

This was a fine championship, and it is ironic that Thomson and Thomas, very close friends, were the two who would decide the outcome. For some years Thomson had tried to persuade the Welshman to play more overseas and gain an international reputation, but Thomas was a quiet and modest man who was never happier than when at home with his family. In any event he did extremely well out of the game, ultimately in golf course architecture in partnership with Peter Alliss.

And so Peter Thomson's remarkable record continued. Since 1952 he had finished 2nd, 2nd, 1st, 1st, 1st, 2nd and 1st.

LEFT: *Peter Thomson celebrates yet another victory in 1958, his fourth in five years.*

First Title for the Little Man in Black

1959

IF THE 1958 OPEN WAS CONSIDERED a vintage championship, the one held at Muirfield in 1959 certainly was not, although Gary Player might not agree! There was a dearth of overseas players, with hardly an American in sight, but this does not detract from what Player achieved. Having come close in previous years, he won the championship aged just 23 and after a first round of 75.

A second-round 71 pulled things around somewhat, but at the start of the final day Player was eight strokes behind the leader, Fred Bullock, the professional from the Prestwick St Ninians Club. However, final rounds of 70 and a 68 that included a six on the final hole saw him home in 284 strokes. Following his closing six Player left the final green totally distraught, thinking his chance of glory had just disappeared, but one by one his challengers fell by the wayside and victory was ultimately his by two strokes from Bullock and Flory van Donck and by three from Syd Scott.

Their efforts were excellent, but mention must also be made of three amateurs who put up outstanding performances. Walker Cup player and Scotsman Reid Jack finished joint fifth, just four strokes behind Player, while Michael Bonallack, who over the next eleven years would win the Amateur Championship on five occasions, finished tied for eleventh place.

One stroke behind Bonallack was another famous amateur, Guy Wolstenholme, thanks to a holed two-iron on the 72nd hole!

Player's performance was remarkable in that he improved his score with every round – 75, 71, 70 and 68. It was only the fourth, and remains the last occasion when the champion has achieved such a feat.

And so, at the end of the Fifties, a new star had arrived on the scene. Now, as the Sixties dawned, the oldest of golf's major championships was about to be given a massive injection of glamour and prestige.

RIGHT: *A distraught Gary Player is consoled by his wife Vivienne having taken six on the final hole at Muirfield. His fears that he had thrown away the championship were later dispelled when Flory Van Donck and Fred Bullock faltered over the closing holes.*

THE CENTENARY OF THE OPEN CHAMPIONSHIP

100

Played over

THE OLD COURSE
ST ANDREWS

Monday 4th July to Friday 8th July

1960

THE ROYAL & ANCIENT GOLF CLUB
OF ST ANDREWS

OFFICIAL PROGRAMME: TWO SHILLINGS & SIXPENCE

ARNOLD PALMER
REVITALIZES
THE CHAMPIONSHIP

1960–1962

T HE GOLFING SENSATION of the late 1950s, Arnold Palmer brought to the game a new sense of dash and excitement. His play was aggressive and swashbuckling and the crowds flocked in their thousands to watch him. The combination of televised sport, the business skills of American lawyer Mark McCormack and the charisma of Palmer suddenly made golf a big attraction.

In 1960 Palmer won the Masters and the US Open and then travelled to Portmarnock in Ireland, where he and Sam Snead won the Canada Cup for the United States. He then moved over to St Andrews for his first Open Championship and failed by just one stroke after a last-round 68 to tie with Kel Nagle of Australia. He returned the following year to win at Birkdale in foul weather conditions and successfully defended his title at Troon in 1962 with a then record-breaking score of 276.

His presence was enormous and his influence such that he persuaded other top American players to travel over and compete in the Open and revive an event that had begun to flag slightly. It was not long before he had helped restore the tournament to its premier position in world golf.

LEFT: *The year 1960 saw the centenary of the Open Championship be celebrated at St Andrews.*

RIGHT: *Arnold Palmer and his wife Winnie celebrate his first Open triumph at Royal Birkdale in 1961. By now he had two Masters and one US Open title but a US PGA title always eluded him (he was runner-up on three occasions).*

1960

Nagle and Palmer Fight Out Centenary Open

THE 1960 CENTENARY OPEN was played, appropriately, at St Andrews, and the Royal & Ancient were determined to make it a special occasion. Despite it being the Centenary Open, with increased prize money, including a first prize of £1,250, the American entry was hardly larger than usual. When one considers that the equivalent for winning the Masters that year was $17,500 and the US Open $14,400, it is hardly surprising.

The good news was that Arnold Palmer, who had just won the Masters and the US Open, did make the trip and came very close to winning at his first attempt. From South Africa came Harold Henning with defending champion Gary Player, while the Australian challenge was led as usual by Peter Thomson and the experienced Kel Nagle.

After two rounds, however, the lead was held by the Argentinian Roberto de Vicenzo, who had already featured strongly in Open championships and would do so again in many more. Thanks to two fine 67s he led by two strokes from Nagle, and next, but seven behind de Vicenzo, were Palmer, Thomson and Sebastian Miguel. In his second round the Argentinian had nothing more than a four on his card – quite an achievement around the Old Course with its enormous greens.

RIGHT: *Spectators run for shelter during a deluge of rain at St Andrews as water cascades down the steps outside the Royal and Ancient clubhouse.*

1960

LEFT: *A smiling Kel Nagle holds the Open trophy and a specially commissioned minature created to celebrate the Centenary of the Open Championship.*

The third and supposedly final day provided drama when early in the fourth round the heavens opened, the course was completely flooded and the officials were quick to declare that play was abandoned for the day. Within minutes of course the sun came out and most of the water drained away!

To everyone's great relief and delight the Saturday dawned bright and sunny and the fourth round got under way. A third-round 75 had meant that de Vicenzo had lost his lead to Nagle, who now led on 207 by two strokes, with Palmer a further two behind.

In the final round Britain's Bernard Hunt returned a superb 66 for a total of 282, but with the three leaders all out in 34 his score did not look quite good enough. Palmer played a faultless back nine and with a birdie at the 18th was round in 68 for a total of 279, three less than de Vicenzo who had faltered on the turn for home.

Playing just behind, Nagle knew exactly what was required – two fours to win. Having played short in two at the 17th, he was left with a ten-foot putt for his par and bravely holed it despite the cheers for Palmer's closing birdie still ringing in his ears. At the 18th he made no mistakes and victory was his by a single stroke.

Nagle's victory was a somewhat surprising one, mainly one suspects because little had been seen of him in the British Isles. He was in fact a fine player who saw much success at home in Australia and especially in New Zealand, where he won the Open title on seven occasions. He also partnered Peter Thomson to victory in the World (formerly Canada) Cup in Montreal in 1954, and again in Melbourne in 1959.

Nagle became a regular visitor to Britain and recorded further victories in other events. In 1965 he tied Gary Player for the US Open but lost the play-off by three strokes. He will be remembered as a solid and consistent player, a great putter and above all an extremely pleasant man.

1961 *Palmer Takes Stormy Championship*

~

FOR SOME REASON the 1961 Open at Royal Birkdale was not one of the happiest in the championship's history. Wild weather before the championship did not help, causing much destruction to various marquees and temporary buildings, and in general arrangements did not go quite to plan.

It did, however, see the first success in the championship of Arnold Palmer, something that had seemed almost inevitable after his excellent performance in the 1960 Open.

When play got under way on the first day the wind had subsided and fine 68s were recorded by Dai Rees of Wales, Harold Henning and the holder Kel Nagle. But by the second day the wind had returned and Peter Thomson's 72 would be the lowest score of the day. Palmer followed up his opening 70 with a 73 that included a seven, a fine round considering he was out in the worst of the weather.

Another stormy night saw many of the temporary buildings blown away, and as at St Andrews the previous year, play was abandoned for the day.

When play resumed the following day Rees promptly started with a seven that did nothing for his chances, but he stuck to it and finished bravely in 71. By now

RIGHT: *South African Harold Henning, a regular Open competitor for more than 25 years, plays to the 13th hole at Birkdale in 1961. He finished third in 1960 and again in 1970, both at St Andrews.*

however, he had been overhauled by Palmer who returned a fine 69. A 67, the lowest score of the week, brought the Irishman Christy O'Connor into contention, just three behind Palmer.

Again in the afternoon Rees struggled on the way out, but a three at the 15th and a four at the 16th kept his hopes alive. The destiny of the championship lay between him and Palmer, but despite a wonderful three by Rees at the 470-yard final hole Palmer crept home by a single stroke.

Dai Rees had an incredible Open record going back to 1935. He was joint runner-up to Hogan at Carnoustie in 1953 and also second to Thomson in 1954, again at Birkdale, but this was to be his last chance of victory. He had an enormous enthusiasm for the game and was extremely fit. This was reflected by his winning of the 1969 Professional Matchplay, 33 years after reaching his first final! He was in nine Ryder Cup teams, five as captain – a remarkable record – and in 1967 was PGA captain and was voted the BBC Sports Personality of the Year.

The Open of 1961 may have appeared to be a somewhat subdued championship, but it was memorable for being Palmer's first victory and it heralded the beginning of a resurgence and 'modernization' of the event. Arnold Palmer's influence on the event should not be underestimated.

ABOVE: *Arnold Palmer in action at Royal Birkdale. Note the upside down scoreboard that uses the old style method with players' scores compared to 'level fours'.*

1962

Huge Crowds Watch Palmer Break All Records

TROON IN 1962 SAW THE START of a new era of the championship. The whole event was much larger, more attention was paid to the requirements and demands of both players and spectators, and thanks to Arnold Palmer more Americans made the journey over. Among them were Gene Littler, Phil Rodgers, Sam Snead (now aged 50 and making his first appearance since his win back in 1946), and a young, somewhat beefy-looking man from Ohio with a crew cut, one Jack Nicklaus.

Palmer was considered to be at the peak of his game and in April had won the Masters for a third time, but he had just lost to Nicklaus in a play-off for the US Open at Oakmont. Aged just 22, Nicklaus appeared to have the golfing world at his feet, but his first Open was not a happy one and after an opening round of 80 (including a ten at the Railway Hole 11th) and a last round of 79 he finished on 305 for 34th place.

Palmer was in complete control of this championship throughout. Rounds of 71 and 69 gave him a two-stroke lead over Thomson, and after a third round of 67 he was five clear of the field. The final round became a victory march as he was cheered home by his 'army' of devoted fans. The margin of victory was eventually six strokes over Kel Nagle and his record total of 276 was one that would stand until 1977. Brian Huggett of Wales and Phil Rodgers shared third place some 13 strokes behind Palmer!

This was an Open where the course was baked hard and the ball ran for miles, seeming to bounce at random in any direction, for rabbits had destroyed the fairways in the weeks prior to the championship. The course was without doubt unfair and not in a good enough condition for such an event, but despite nearly going home after the practice rounds Palmer took up the challenge and annihilated the rest of the field. The size of the crowds swarming over the course to see him play led to the roping off of Open courses in future years to keep control. This was Palmer's second and final Open success, and no one did more than he did to restore the championship to its undisputed status as the world's most prestigious golfing event.

On a light-hearted tack, Phil Rodgers required a four on the final hole to take third place alone, but he saw his second shot bounce through the green, thump against a spectator and land in a tankard of beer! His request for a free drop, having claimed that his ball was lying in casual beer, was denied as both the spectator and the tankard were standing out of bounds!

THE ERA OF NICKLAUS, PLAYER AND TREVINO

1963-1974

THE EARLY 1960S SAW TWO PLAYERS challenge Arnold Palmer for supremacy in the world of golf. Gary Player had been winning events around the world as far back as 1956, including the Open at Muirfield in 1959. His sheer determination and relentless drive for success have made him one of the game's legends, and there are few harder-practising or physically fitter players in the game. The rewards have been huge, including three Open Championships, three US Masters, the US Open and two US PGA victories, as well as over 100 tournament successes around the world.

The presence of Gary Player was to become a permanent feature of the Open and the fact that his three victories have all come in different decades underlines his fitness, dedication and loyalty to the event.

The second player to challenge Palmer's dominance in the early 1960s is arguably the greatest golfer in history – Jack Nicklaus. The statistics alone make it difficult to refute this claim. His record of 18 major victories is seven more than anyone else. He has been runner-up in 19 other Majors, more than double any other player, and by 1986, when he had competed in some 100 Majors, he had finished in the first three on no less than 46 occasions. His record in the Open is quite phenomenal despite the fact that he has won the championship just three times! In the 17 championships between 1963 and 1979 he finished in the first three on 14 occasions.

As his domination of the game increased, so did his popularity with the crowds. In the early days, with a crew-cut hairstyle, and carrying excess weight, he was not popular with 'Arnie's Army', who saw him as a threat to Palmer's supremacy. Over the years, however, he has become respected as the greatest player of the modern game and possibly of all time. There is no finer ambassador for the game of golf worldwide, and to be present at the 18th green when Nicklaus walks up the final fairway of a Major Championship is one of sport's most emotional moments.

The late 1960s saw the emergence of a third player, Lee Trevino, who brought colour, humour and a sense of the unorthodox to the game. The son of a Mexican grave-digger, he had come from the humblest of backgrounds. When, in 1968, he won the US Open at The Oak Hill Country Club in New York, he became the first player in history to win a Major with four rounds each under 70.

At St Andrews in 1970, partnering Doug Sanders in the last round, he missed out only by two strokes, taking 77, but the following year in a dramatic finish at Royal Birkdale he recorded his first Open success. At Muirfield in 1972 he successfully defended his title after a titanic last-round struggle with Nicklaus and Tony Jacklin. For many years this most genial of characters brought drama, humour and excitement to golf and will go down in history as one of the game's greatest players and fiercest competitors.

Following the years of Arnold Palmer these three players dominated the Open for many years until the emergence in 1975 of Tom Watson.

1963   *Left-Handed Charles Takes Title to New Zealand*

FOLLOWING THE RESURGENCE of the championship after Palmer's consecutive victories, the 1963 Open at Royal Lytham had a new look to it. There was a much larger Trade Exhibition area, a new system of exemption from qualifying for the leading players, and also a far stronger overseas challenge. As well as past champions Player, Nagle and Thomson, from America came Palmer, Nicklaus (having just won his first Masters) and Rodgers again, from France there was Jean Garaialde and from New Zealand Bob Charles, who had come a distant fifth the previous year.

With the exception of Palmer, who had a poor week, the overseas players dominated. Of the home players only Ireland's Christy O'Connor was to finish in the top ten.

On the first morning a new nine-hole record for the Open was set when both Peter Thomson and Tom Haliburton, the professional at Wentworth, played the first nine in 29 strokes. Despite this, after two rounds it was Phil Rodgers who led, by a stroke from Peter Thomson, three from Nicklaus, four from Nagle with Charles a further stroke back.

On the following morning Charles played the round of the week, his 66 including just 26 putts. Having trailed Rodgers by five, he was suddenly in the lead on his own, one ahead of Thomson.

In the afternoon Thomson played what was probably his worst round in an Open when in a challenging position, his 78 leaving him eight strokes adrift at the end of the day. Otherwise all the leading challengers played fine last rounds. Nicklaus, aided by an eagle three at the 7th, led after ten holes, and when he hit a majestic two-iron just 15 feet from the pin at the 15th he looked favourite for the title. But incredibly he three-putted and despite a birdie at the next hole he finished with two fives against a par of 4, 4.

Charles and Rodgers, playing together in the final group, were then left on the 72nd tee level, both requiring par fours to edge past Nicklaus by a single stroke. Rodgers made sure of his four first, and then Charles holed from about four feet for his. Their score of 277 was just one stroke outside Palmer's record score of the previous year.

And so they returned the following day to decide the winner by way of a 36-hole play-off. (It was the last year, happily, that this format was used.) With another display of precision putting Charles's two-round total of 140 was eight too good for the American. Having single-putted 11 greens in the morning he had a three-

ABOVE: *Jack Nicklaus in action. By the time of the 1963 Open he had already won the US Open the previous year and the Masters earlier in 1963.*

1963

LEFT: *Bob Charles drives from the 15th tee during his 36-hole play-off victory over American Phil Rodgers. Charles remains the only left-hander to win the title.*

stroke lead at lunch, and although Rodgers managed to close the gap to just one early in the afternoon, his game fell apart and he ended with a 76. So, for the first and as yet only time the Open was won by a left-hander, and a New Zealander.

Charles's career has been extraordinarily long when one considers that he won the New Zealand Open for the first of three occasions in 1954 as an amateur and is still plucking many thousands of dollars from the US Seniors Tour. He was to finish second in two further Open Championships, and other notable victories were the Piccadilly World Matchplay at Wentworth in 1969, the John Player Classic at Turnberry in 1972 and the Seniors British Open in 1989.

Above all he will be remembered for his silky putting stroke. At times in his heyday he looked likely to hole any putt he addressed and when asked who was the finest putter of their lifetime many highly respected golf aficionados reply without hesitation with the name of Bob Charles.

1964 'Champagne' Tony Wins in Style

Tᴏɴʏ ʟᴇᴍᴀ ᴄᴀᴍᴇ ꜰʀᴏᴍ ʜᴜᴍʙʟᴇ ʙᴇɢɪɴɴɪɴɢꜱ in San Francisco, the son of a Portugese labourer who died when his son was just three years old. Like many other poor young American boys Lema earned a few dollars as a caddie at the local public course. In his teens he signed up to serve in the US Marines and went off to fight in the grim, bloody campaign in Korea.

On returning home he felt the lure of golf again and it was not long before he was appointed professional at a local course close to San Francisco. Two unsuccessful years on the circuit followed and then out of the blue he won a

tournament in 1962, and after buying champagne for the Press entourage the nickname of 'Champagne' Tony stuck.

Suddenly Lema became a big money earner on the tour and was runner-up in the Masters in 1963. Then in a very short space of time in 1964 he won three tournaments in America, the last of them, the Cleveland Open, in the week preceding the Open Championship.

It was this success that brought Lema to St Andrews for the Open, having never previously competed in Europe, let alone having ever played a links course before! Landing a mere 36 hours before the championship, he managed just nine holes of practice and a walk of the course before taking it on. Hardly ideal preparation for an Open Championship!

A wind of fifty miles an hour on the first day did not make matters any easier, but somehow he returned a score of 73, a remarkable achievement. His putting, on greens unlike anything he had encountered in America, was miraculous.

On the second day, with just a little more knowledge of the course, and with the help of local caddie 'Tip' Anderson, whom Palmer had previously employed and recommended, Lema shot a 68 to take the lead. He had a two-stroke cushion over Englishman Harry Weetman, with Christy O'Connor and Australian Bruce Devlin a further stroke back. By now he was being talked of as a serious potential winner, with many St Andrews locals shaking their heads in disbelief that anyone could play such golf on their first visit.

The third round, played on the Friday morning, belonged to Nicklaus with a 66. However, Lema was out in 36 and, seeing that Nicklaus had gone to the turn in 32, in his own words, 'decided I had to get up a bit of steam'! Five threes followed on the back nine and he was home in 32 himself for a 68. So Nicklaus, despite his wonderful score, gained just two strokes, and although he entered the final round as Lema's closest pursuer, was still a massive seven strokes behind.

Lema made no mistake in the afternoon with a round of 70, and despite superb rounds of 68 and 67 from Nicklaus and de Vicenzo respectively, Lema was champion with five strokes to spare. (At one stage, however, Nicklaus had made up the seven strokes by which he trailed.)

Long before he holed out on the final green the champagne was on its way to the Press Tent and forty bottles later the scribes were voting Tony Lema a great champion and a wonderful fellow!

He made a spirited defence of his title the following year at Royal Birkdale and was then involved in one of the most dramatic matches ever known in the World Matchplay Championship at Wentworth, when he lost to Gary Player at the 37th after having been seven up on the 20th tee. Despite this he showed tremendous dignity and sportsmanship in defeat.

Tragedy struck in 1966 when Lema, his wife Betty and their travelling companions were all killed in a private plane when it crashed on landing in Illinois – ironically, on a golf course.

There is no knowing how many more Major championships this most affable man could have won. His victory at St Andrews will go down as one of the most remarkable in Open history.

ABOVE: *Tony Lema displays perfect balance as Henry Cotton looks on.*

1965

Thomson's Fifth and Finest

PROBABLY THE STRONGEST INTERNATIONAL FIELD at the time assembled at Royal Birkdale for the 1965 Open. Following the dreary and disappointing affair of 1961 the club made a superb effort for this championship and succeeded in producing a memorable week.

Again the Tented Village had grown, and now television towers were to be seen dotted around the course, and with new communications systems in place the ever-increasing Press corps were able to have information relayed back to them.

As happens so often at Birkdale the wind blew for much of the week, and in these conditions Peter Thomson was at his best. He had a simple and repetitive swing and no matter how hard the wind blew he retained his balance and rhythm.

Tony Lema opened the defence of his title with a splendid 68, one of only two sub-70 rounds of the day, and after two days the familiar names of Lema, Thomson, de Vicenzo, Devlin, O'Connor, Palmer and Nagle were all at the top of the leader board.

A less familiar name on the leader board was that of Welshman Brian Huggett, who had been second in 1962 and 14th the following year. A dogged, gutsy player, he had started with rounds of 73 and 68 and despite a third-round 76 that contained four sixes he was still in contention entering the final round. The lead had changed hands 11 times in the third round and ultimately lay with Thomson on 214, followed by Lema and Devlin one behind, with O'Connor, Palmer and de Vicenzo a further stroke back and Huggett, Yorkshireman Lionel Platts, Spain's Sebastian Miguel and Nagle just one behind them.

After 13 holes of the final round Thomson still led by one from his playing partner Lema. O'Connor then completed his round in 71 for a total of 287, soon matched by Huggett who had recovered well from the morning with a more than respectable three-under-par 70. Try as he might, Lema could make no further progress and Thomson stood on the 17th tee requiring par figures of five and four to be almost certain of the title. An immaculate birdie four immediately followed after his second shot hit the pin, and he made no mistake at the last with a cast-iron four. Lema's challenge had disappeared completely with an awful six at the last. So Thomson was champion again, by two strokes, and had won the championship five times in 12 years – a remarkable achievement.

Whatever the sceptics may say about his victories in the 1950s when international competition was not that strong, no one can question the value of his victory of 1965, when he took on and beat the world's greatest players, including the finest of the new generation of stars.

RIGHT: *Peter Thomson displays the skill that made him a great champion. His fifth Open success at Royal Birkdale in 1965 was considered his greatest feat as he took on and beat a truly international field.*

1966

The Nicklaus Years Begin

ANOTHER QUALITY INTERNATIONAL FIELD contested the 95th Open Championship at Muirfield and they were blessed with a week of fine weather. For the first time the event was extended to four days, from Wednesday to Saturday, which resulted in a larger crowd, and the new format was also popular with the players. The prize money was again raised – this time the champion was to collect £2,100.

Another change was that Muirfield's fairways had been narrowed down and the rough had been allowed to grow knee deep. It was utterly brutal, resulting in much high scoring.

Nicklaus, who earlier in the year had won his third Masters, took control with rounds of 70 and 67. But a third-round 75 left him trailing his American compatriot Phil Rodgers by two after Rodgers had compiled a 70 made up of halves of 40 out and 30 home!

One behind Nicklaus after the third round was another American, the colourful and flamboyant Doug Sanders (dressed this day entirely in tangerine!) who four years later was involved in one of the championship's most dramatic finishes. A further stroke behind were Arnold Palmer and Dave Thomas, who had so nearly won in 1958.

On the final day Nicklaus charged to the turn in 33 while Rodgers took 37, and with Thomas, Palmer and Sanders all out in 34 the lead had turned upside down. Rodgers then fell out of contention completely with his second six of the round, and Palmer did likewise, after getting tangled up in the rough on the 10th and taking a seven. Sanders, having chipped in at the 9th from 60 yards for an eagle, spoilt it all by visiting the rough on the 11th and a six went down on his card.

Suddenly the only challenger to Nicklaus was Thomas who, with two twos and a three on the back nine, was home in 69, the best score of the day, for a total of 283.

Nicklaus required a birdie and a par to win and did so magnificently. Neither his birdie four at the 17th nor his par four at the last were in doubt, and he walked from the final green as champion by a single stroke from Thomas and Sanders, who had made a gallant recovery following his six at the 11th.

Nicklaus had been seen as a future winner of the Open for many years and no one was surprised at his victory. After all, this was already his sixth Major victory at the age of just 26. His win completed victory in all four Majors in a space of just five years and meant that he had joined Sarazen, Hogan and Player as the only players to have won all four – a record that still stands.

Jacklin the Hero

1969

THE BRITISH GOLFING PUBLIC had already witnessed 17 consecutive Open victories by overseas players, but finally in 1969 they had a British victory to celebrate.

Tony Jacklin was born in 1944 in Scunthorpe, in the north of England. He was introduced to golf at the age of nine and very soon his great talent was evident. He was also a very determined young man whose heart was set on golfing fame and fortune.

Success soon followed and in 1961, aged 17, Jacklin went to Potters Bar Golf Club in Middlesex ito work with and be guided by the professional, Bill Shankland. His first big victory came in 1967 at Royal St George's, when he won the Dunlop Masters with a last-round 64 which included the first televised hole in one, on the 16th. In America the next year he won the Jacksonville Open.

Jacklin had already competed in the Open for some years and had been making steady progress. In 1967 he finished fifth to de Vicenzo at Hoylake. Many thought that victory one day was inevitable.

And so to Royal Lytham. Jacklin had the perfect start with a birdie two at the 1st and completed his round in 68. This was two more than Bob Charles, however, who was continuing with the quality of golf he had displayed six years earlier in his successful Open year, also at Lytham.

Charles followed with a 69, Jacklin a 70, and so at halfway the scores were: Charles 135, O'Connor 136 (his second round of 65 the lowest of the week) and Jacklin on 138. A host of familiar names such as Nicklaus, Player, Thomson, de Vicenzo and Casper were not far behind.

On the Friday Charles's putter began to let him down. The usual magic just wasn't there and a 75 was the result. Consequently this blew the championship wide open, and at the end of the day Jacklin's 70 left him at the top of the leader board. Two behind him were Charles and O'Connor, with Thomson and de Vicenzo a further stroke away and Nicklaus lurking nearby following a third-round 68. The scene was set for a fascinating last day, with real belief among the home crowd that Jacklin would be good enough to repel his challengers and capture an Open victory.

He could not have asked for a better start. Paired with Charles, who dropped a stroke on the opening hole, Jacklin birdied the 3rd and 4th. Out in 33, he had extended his lead to four and, despite Charles gaining strokes on the 10th and 13th, he stood on the 18th tee with a two-stroke advantage.

ABOVE: *Tony Jacklin in full flow during his final round. His welcome victory finally brought to an end 18 years without a British win.*

1969

BELOW: *The final putt goes in and a new British sporting hero is born. The following June Tony Jacklin took the US Open title at Hazeltine by seven strokes and in doing so joined Harry Vardon and Ted Ray as the only British players to have won both titles.*

He wasted no time and any nerves were well hidden as he drilled a magnificent drive long and straight down the middle. Charles played his second shot to the green first and a wonderful stroke it was.

The tension was absolutely electric – Charles could still make a birdie and Jacklin could take five. But again without much delay his stroke was perfect and his ball flew straight like an arrow to the green, finishing a yard or so nearer the hole than Charles's.

At last the tension was over and the crowd's relief opened out. Jacklin was mobbed and finally emerged carrying one of his shoes that had come off in all the chaos!

Charles's birdie putt just failed and Jacklin had the luxury of three putts for victory. Two were sufficient and a new British sporting hero was born! From that moment Jacklin's life would never be the same again.

The scenes that followed were ecstatic ones, and those who were present or those fans who watched the excitement unravel on television will surely never forget Saturday, 12 July 1969, the day that Tony Jacklin restored faith and hope in British golf.

It was around this time that the renowned Bollinger champagne company first began its high profile association with sporting events and in particular with the Open Championship, a highly successful association that has lasted for over 30 years.

Following a visit to an earlier golfing event, Anthony Leschallas, then Director of Mentzendorff, Bollinger champagne's sole agents in the UK, came up with the idea of creating a Bollinger Tent.

1969

The House of Bollinger was founded in 1829 by Jacques Bollinger and the control of the business has since been passed on from generation to generation. The company owns some of the finest vineyards in the champagne region and has acquired a worldwide reputation for quality and style. Such is their commitment to the art of making champagne that only grapes from their own vineyards or from a select number of growers with whom they have worked for many years are used in their 'cuvee'. This means that only a finite number of bottles can be produced each year and consequently fluctuations in demand from around the world cannot always be met. Such high standards and a refusal to bow to industry pressure make Bollinger what it is today and an ideal addition to the Open Championship.

In the mid 1960s the Open was not the major event it is today and there were only two marquees of any note: the Golf Illustrated Tent and a catering tent run by Smallmans.

When the first Bollinger Tent was erected at Royal Lytham in 1969 it was hardly recognizable as that of today. There was barely room to swing a cat but this was not a problem as hardly anyone entered the tent during the whole week. Leschallas' temporary staff, a Jamaican nightclub barman and a female student from Blackpool, were not over-exercised. Drinking champagne at sporting events was unheard of and at £3 a bottle only two cases were sold in the entire week.

To console himself, Leschallas and his friends sat around on tables and chairs outside the tent and made sure that little of the stock needed to be returned to the London office at the end of the Championship.

By the time of the 1970 Open, Bollinger's situation had improved a little. Despite the tent being erected out on the New Course and with poor weather, the sales for that week at St Andrews were some 200 bottles sold at £4.50 per bottle.

The 1971 championship at Royal Birkdale saw a sudden transformation in Bollinger's fortune. For the first time the the tent was pitched close to the 1st tee and sales subsequently rocketed. Such was the demand for Bollinger that staff had to be sent out to local stockists to ensure continuity of supply. From sales of a mere 200 bottles the previous year, the thirsty folk of Birkdale now consumed in excess of 100 cases.

The Bollinger Tent had suddenly become a popular social meeting point. Even competitors called in for a glass occasionally, a rarity nowadays.

In the early 1970s the days of corporate hospitality were unheard of and Leschallas, soon to be joined in the business by his son Simon, had successfully cornered the market.

Bollinger's sales figures for the Open are remarkable. The record for a single day so far is held at Royal Troon in 1997 (it was a hot day!) when the Mentzendorff team opened 1100 bottles of champagne. Some 4000 bottles were opened at Royal Birkdale in 1998. An impressive five and a half tons of ice and some 10,000 glasses are used each year. In 1969 just three people were required to staff the tent. It now requires nine. To date Simon Leschallas has been pouring champagne for

1969

his clients at the Open for 21 years. Surely he is one of the Open Championship's most loyal staff!

Much has happened within the red and white stripes of The Bollinger Tent or 'Bolly Tent' as it is affectionately known. Business deals have been struck, lifelong friendships made and much laughter and fun had. It has become a familiar and focal point for many regular visitiors to the Open and a welcome point for many a first time visitor! It has also witnessed a number of memorable and unique events. There has been the Extraordinary General (and not entirely sober) Meeting of the One Armed Golfing Society; a robbery ending with the villains being chased across the 17th fairway at Muirfield, and much more.

As the Open has grown to become one of the world's great sporting events so has the success of Bollinger champagne. Long may it continue to be a feature at the championship.

BELOW: *The Bollinger Tent. Since 1969 it has been an institution and second home to many at the Open.*

Tragedy for Sanders

1970

T HE 1970 OPEN AT ST ANDREWS will always be remembered for one thing – Doug Sanders's missed putt on the final green – but so much more happened in the week that made this an outstanding championship.

A hugely strong field gathered to challenge at the home of golf. Nicklaus, Sanders, Palmer, Player, Trevino, Casper and de Vicenzo were all present from abroad, and the home challenge was led by defending champion Tony Jacklin.

The start was delayed by mist, but once it had cleared conditions were ideal and two English players led the way. Tommy Horton scored a 66 and Neil Coles a 65 that set a new course record and matched the championship record. As Coles walked up the 18th fairway seven under par, Jacklin was just starting the defence of his title. Undaunted by Coles's score he started with three consecutive birdies and had others at the 5th and 7th. Needing a four at the short par four 9th for an outward 31, his pitch shot looked strong but second bounce struck the pin and dropped straight into the hole for an eagle two – out in 29 and already seven under par!

Another birdie soon followed, but the weather was deteriorating rapidly. Suddenly a cloudburst erupted and within minutes the course was unplayable. By this time Jacklin had hit his second shot at the 14th into a gorse bush and moments later play was abandoned for the day. When he returned to complete his round in the morning the magic had gone, and after dropped shots at the 16th and 17th he finished in 67. One will never know what score he might have achieved but for the storm.

Other fine first-round scores had been achieved. South Africa's Harold Henning recorded a 67, and Nicklaus, Palmer, Trevino and Sanders all scored 68. Sanders's score was a fine effort considering his second to the 1st finished in the Swilcan Burn and he started the championship with a six. A second successive 68 gave Trevino the lead after two rounds, one clear of Nicklaus and three ahead of Jacklin, Sanders, Henning, Coles, Horton and Clive Clark.

On Friday, the third day, the sun shone but the wind blew stronger and scoring was tougher. Peter Oosterhuis, a 22-year-old English professional with a promising career ahead of him, suddenly appeared on the scene with a superb 69 and finished the day on five under par, a wonderful achievement. Trevino and Jacklin, playing together in the final pair, both birdied the 1st and 18th to finish with 72 and 73 respectively. And so, entering the final round, Trevino led by two from Nicklaus, Sanders and Jacklin, with Oosterhuis and Coles a further stroke behind.

ABOVE: *Doug Sanders making possibly the most famous miss in Open history.*

The fourth day brought glimpses of sunshine mixed with gusts of wind and one by one most of the leaders fell away. Trevino three-putted twice on the outward nine and despite a birdie at the last hole he finished on 77, to be just too far away on 285. His total was matched by Harold Henning, but ultimately it was left to Sanders and Nicklaus to determine the outcome of the championship. On the 14th Sanders missed a putt from four feet which would have given him a two-stroke lead that might have been enough. On the 18th green Nicklaus just missed his birdie and walked off disconsolately, convinced that his chance of victory had gone.

Sanders, playing just behind in the final group, then put his second to the 17th in the Road bunker. Under extraordinary pressure he played the stroke of a lifetime and blasted the ball out adjacent to the hole. In went the tap-in and he now needed just a four at the last for victory.

A fine drive down went down the middle of the fairway. By now Sanders looked extremely stressed and before playing his approach walked all the way to the pin to survey the shot ahead. Surely this only added to the pressure. He elected to play a high pitch and, making sure he avoided the Valley of Sin, he over-hit his shot, ending some 35 feet past the pin. His first putt finished some three to three and a half feet from the hole and he was now left with a downhill left-to-right putt to win the Open!

He stood over his ball, then suddenly bent down to pick up a blade of grass. The crowd gasped, Trevino his playing partner appealed for quiet and finally, after what seemed an age, he stabbed his putt past the right side of the hole.

Sanders was distraught. His chance for outright victory had gone and now he had to play an 18-hole play-off the following day against arguably the world's leading player. It is rumoured that he spent much of that night lying on his back in a field looking to the stars contemplating what might have been!

The next day saw Nicklaus take control early on and after four holes he led by two. At the 5th, he seemed to be in terrible trouble and facing a six or seven, he played what he later described as the shot of a lifetime to three feet and escaped with a par five.

After 13 holes Nicklaus led by four and Sanders' hopes, it appeared, had gone. Suddenly, however, he birdied the 14th and 15th and at the 16th Nicklaus failed to make par. They both played wonderful second shots to the heart of the 17th green and the hole was halved in four, leaving Nicklaus one ahead playing the last hole.

Sanders, with the honour, drove far down the middle of the fairway and finished only just short of The Valley of Sin. Nicklaus then removed his sweater and unleashed an enormous stroke that ran right through the green, ending up in a nasty grassy spot on the steep bank at the back. Sanders played first and ran up a wonderful shot some six feet past the pin. Oh for that shot the day before! Nicklaus then chopped his ball out, which rolled down the hill and finished just further away than Sanders'.

His downhill left-to-right putt for victory seemed to be falling away to the right but at the last moment it fell into the hole! Nicklaus hurled his putter into the air – only just missing Sanders – and finally after five remarkable days he was

ABOVE: *Doug Sanders and Jack Nicklaus on the 1st tee as they start their famous play-off.*

seemed his brave challenge was over. His 66, one of the great last rounds in Open history could so easily have been 62 or 63.

As they approached the 17th tee, Jacklin and Trevino were level, and as at Birkdale the previous year it appeared that after their drives Trevino's hopes had gone. Bunkered from the tee, he finally made the fringe at the back of the green in four. Meanwhile Jacklin was just 30 yards short of the green in two. His run up to 18 feet seemed satisfactory, but then to Jacklin's horror Trevino chipped in yet again!

Shattered, Jacklin put his first putt three feet past and comfortably missed the return. Completely destroyed by Trevino's magic, luck or whatever you wish to call it, he dropped another stroke at the final hole and within the space of minutes the title that was almost certainly his for a second time had gone, as had second place which went to Nicklaus by a stroke.

As they had approached the 17th green Trevino passed Jacklin and said, 'I'm through – it's all yours.' What a cruel and unpredictable game it can be, and many believe that Jacklin never recovered from this experience. He would never challenge seriously again in any Major championship, whereas Trevino went on to capture two US PGA titles.

ABOVE: *The stroke that many feel was the end of Tony Jacklin's career. Moments earlier he looked the champion all over but when Trevino chipped in yet again, Jacklin's heart was broken. He three-putted and lost an almost certain second Open title.*

1973   *Weiskopf Swinging in the Rain*

THE OPEN RETURNED TO TROON in 1973 for the first time since Arnold Palmer destroyed the rest of the field in 1962, and following successive years of glorious weather it was too much to expect a third!

Arguably the strongest field ever had assembled to try to prevent Trevino completing a hat-trick of wins, including Johnny Miller, fresh from his stunning victory in the US Open at Oakmont, where he had sliced through the field with a last-round 63, and Tom Weiskopf, the current World Matchplay Champion.

The round of the first day belonged to Weiskopf, his 68 in the worst of the weather proving the old adage 'practice makes perfect'. He had travelled over early and put in no fewer than eight practice rounds! Just a stroke behind were Nicklaus and fellow American Bert Yancey, with Miller one further away after a 70.

But the highlight of the first day was the sight of 71-year-old Gene Sarazen, on a sentimental journey to the course where he had failed to qualify for the 1923 Open, holing his five-iron tee shot at the famous Postage Stamp 8th. Sadly, the following day, when he holed a bunker shot at the same hole for a two the cameras failed to record it!

The second day started with strong winds blowing straight across the course followed by heavy rain – very heavy rain. Palmer came in with a 76, not a bad score considering he had run up a seven at the Postage Stamp. Brian Barnes returned the joint lowest score of the day, a 67, but otherwise it was the big names that were at the top of the leader board. Weiskopf matched Barnes's 67 to take a three-stroke lead from Miller and Yancey, with Nicklaus a further one behind.

Foul weather continued overnight and into the third day, but some good scores were posted even so. Barnes continued his fine form with a 70 for a three-under-par total of 213 which was matched by Britain's Neil Coles. But at the end of the day it was Miller and Weiskopf, despite playing in lashing rain, who seemed to have the championship between them after rounds of 69 and 71 respectively. Entering the final day Weiskopf was on 206, one ahead of Miller and five ahead of Yancey. Coles was two strokes further back, with Nicklaus even further behind following a 76 and apparently suffering from back trouble.

Almost predictably, it was Nicklaus who made the most significant challenge on the final day. Playing in brighter weather than the last group out, he took his chance and helped by birdies at the first two holes was out in 32. A chip in for a birdie at the 13th followed and a closing birdie from a seemingly impossible position for a round of 65 saw him in the clubhouse as leader on an eight-under total of 280. Coles then followed Nicklaus in with a closing birdie for a fine 66 and a total of 279 to take the lead.

The real battle, however, was with Weiskopf and Miller in the final group. Miller started poorly, dropping two strokes in the first three holes to give Weiskopf a three-shot advantage. Try as he might, Miller could not claw back the deficit, and when he three-putted the 15th the championship was effectively over.

With a closing 70 Weiskopf was champion by three strokes, and his total of 276 matched that of Palmer, also at Troon, but in totally different conditions, 11 years earlier. Remarkably he played the four rounds without three-putting once, and he was the first champion since Henry Cotton in 1934 to lead after all four rounds.

1973

LEFT: *Tom Weiskopf lines up a putt en route to a famous victory at Troon. A majestic swinger of the golf club, Weiskopf led the championship from start to finish, defeating Johnny Miller and Neil Coles by two strokes.*

Weiskopf had always had a somewhat fiery temper, but his father's death just three months earlier seemed to have instilled in him a maturity and determination not previously seen. After this victory, following third place in the US Open only weeks before, further wins seemed imminent, but strangely he won just a handful more events on the US Tour and this was to be his only Major success, although in the Masters he was second on no fewer than four occasions.

He will be remembered above all for having one of the most elegant and classical of swings.

NEIL COLES

A VETERAN OF MORE THAN twenty Open Championships, Coles was a professional who went about his business in a quiet way but at the same time built up a fine record. Five times in the top ten, his best year was 1973 at Troon when a last-round 65 helped him to a share of second place to Tom Weiskopf. A member of seven Ryder Cup teams, Coles would surely have achieved more success abroad if not for his phobia of flying.

1974

Player Wins Third Title with Big Ball

ANOTHER LARGE AND STRONG FIELD gathered for the 1974 Open at Royal Lytham and St Annes, the scene of Tony Jacklin's great victory five years before. This year for the first time the larger 1.68-inch ball, which had already been in use in the United States for many years, was made compulsory. Many of the Americans had previously used the smaller ball when in Britain as it travelled some 15 yards further and was also easier to control in the wind. Having to use the larger ball would probably be an advantage to a good wind player.

Gary Player, having just won his second Masters title, was in the line-up, as was Hale Irwin, who had just taken the US Open title at Winged Foot for his first Major success.

Lytham is not the longest of championship courses but somehow refuses to succumb to many low scores. Much trouble awaits an errant shot, and if the wind blows, as is likely, one is sure to find it over the course of four rounds. It is a tribute to the course that at this championship Gary Player, the eventual winner, was the only player of the top six finishers to break 70.

Over the first two days, in windy conditions, he played out of his skin and his rounds of 69 and 68 gave him a five-stroke lead over Peter Oosterhuis and Bobby Cole, with defending champion Tom Weiskopf seven behind and Nicklaus nine behind. Some said, rather prematurely, that the championship was already over!

Friday, the third day, produced sunshine but the wind still blew. Nicklaus picked up three strokes to par early on but a disappointing finish gave him a 70 for a total of 216 that kept him well in the hunt. Player, meanwhile, faltered on the front nine and when he holed out on the 10th green his entire lead had been lost – Cole having gone out in 34 and then birdied the 10th. But suddenly Cole dropped five strokes over seven holes and there his challenge ended. Player, despite a scrappy 75, ended the day three in front of Oosterhuis and now only four ahead of Nicklaus and five ahead of Hubert Green of the United States.

On a final day full of sunshine Player immediately showed he meant business and birdied the first two holes, eagled the 6th and birdied the 7th! (both par fives) to be out in 32. Nicklaus and Green went to the turn in 34 to stay just in contention, but neither made further progress and both finished on 71, Nicklaus birdying the final hole – by now almost a tradition! Their totals were 287 and 288 respectively. Player's only challenger now was Oosterhuis, but try as he might he just could not close the gap. At the 13th, when it seemed he would reduce the deficit by one, Player promptly chipped in from the back of the green!

BELOW: *Gary Player contemplates putting left-handed to the final green after his approach shot finished lodged against the clubhouse wall.*

He was never really in danger despite minor panics at the final two holes. On the 17th after a pulled second it took several minutes scrambling around in knee-deep rough to find his ball, and an over-strong approach to the final hole resulted in him having to putt left-handed with his ball inches from the clubhouse. The final winning margin was four strokes, and his total of 282 meant he was the only player to break par for the four rounds.

There is no doubting that, with victory both at the Masters and here, 1974 was Gary Player's year. This was his third Open success, each of the three, remarkably, won in different decades – a testament to his dedication, competitiveness and fitness. It is wonderful that some 25 years later he still plays to the highest level with an unquenchable enthusiasm and appetite for the game.

He, Sarazen, Hogan and Nicklaus remain the only players to have won all four Major championships – a record all the more remarkable when one considers how many great players have never achieved it.

ABOVE: *Gary Player's last round 70 secured his third Open title by five strokes from Britain's Peter Oosterhuis. With high finishes in the US Open and US PGA as well as victory in the Masters, 1974 was certainly Player's year.*

THE WATSON YEARS
1975–1983

J ACK NICKLAUS'S DOMINANCE of the game was challenged and ultimately seized by Tom Watson in the late 1970s. They had some titanic struggles, none more dramatic than in the 1977 Open at Turnberry and in the 1982 US Open at Pebble Beach.

In 1975 Watson arrived in Britain for the Open Championship at Carnoustie and became only the third American after Ben Hogan and Tony Lema to win at the first attempt. He fell in love with British links courses, enjoying having to manufacture shots rather than just hit the ball high and straight at the pin.

His Open record over the following years was extraordinary, with further victories in 1977, 1980, 1982 and 1983. At St Andrews in 1984 he let a record-equalling sixth title slip away and this seemed to mark a turning-point in his career. At the peak of his career he was a phenomenal putter but, as with so many players, he began to suffer problems.

He remains a regular competitor in the Open Championship and still seeks that elusive sixth title. He has a huge respect for the traditions and history of the game, and rarely has there been a more popular or gracious Open Champion.

LEFT: *Tom Watson celebrates a fifth Open title at Royal Birkdale in 1983 with a slightly damaged Claret Jug following a small slip up!*

RIGHT: *Huge crowds follow Tom Watson and Jack Nicklaus in their epic duel at Turnberry in 1977. The view from the majestic Turnberry Hotel is one of golf's most spectacular sights.*

1975

The Watson Years Begin

ABOVE: *Tom Watson's putt for a birdie drops on the 72nd green to secure a play-off with Australian Jack Newton.*

THE 1975 CHAMPIONSHIP was held at Carnoustie, a course with a fiercely tough reputation. In its previous Open in 1968 the top eight finishers had managed just two sub-70 rounds between them. This time, unusually, for three days there was no wind and the world's leading players made a nonsense of the par of 72. However, the three most recent champions, Player, Weiskopf and Trevino, were all over par in the first round and never recovered.

The first day belonged to Peter Oosterhuis with a 68, but after two rounds the lead was with David Huish, known to the locals as the pro from nearby North Berwick, but totally unknown to the world's leading players. Having survived a sudden death play-off in pre-qualifying, he now led the Open Championship by two strokes after rounds of 69 and 67! Sadly, closing rounds of 76 and 80 saw him slip to joint 37th, but for two days he had been a national hero. After his 68 Oosterhuis went to the turn in 31 on the second day but then fell away with a back nine of 39 which ultimately probably cost him the title.

The third day again saw no wind and the leading players made the most of it with some stunning scoring. Bobby Cole, who had won the Amateur Championship here in 1966 at the age of 18, had a second consecutive 66 and took the lead on 12 under par. One stroke behind was a young Australian, Jack Newton, whose 65 matched the championship record score set by Henry Cotton way back in 1934. Lining up behind were all the big guns: Miller, Irwin, John Mahaffey (runner-up in the US Open a few weeks before), Nicklaus and Tom Watson. The 25-year-old Watson had a big reputation at home in the States, but for two seasons had sometimes let the big prizes slip away from him when within his grasp. Rather cruelly he had been labelled a 'choker', rather an unkind tag for someone who had won the Byron Nelson Classic earlier in the year with a closing 65. He had never played links golf in the British Isles, and had hardly a practice round, but suddenly found himself just three strokes off the lead entering the final day!

On the final day the wind blew at last and Carnoustie lived up to its reputation. Only Watson of the leaders matched the par of 35 on the front nine, but then promptly three-putted the 10th, 11th and 12th. In fact only one player broke 70 for the day – Bob Charles, champion as far back as 1963, with a 69. The next best score was 71.

Nicklaus finished with a 72, having missed a host of birdie chances, and when he walked off the 72nd green at eight under par his rueful look at the scoreboard suggested that it was not quite enough. How accurate he proved to be.

1977

Surely the championship was now his. But no, Nicklaus was a true champion, and he proceeded to play one of the most remarkable shots, smashing at the ball with an eight-iron, somehow getting the ball on to the edge of the putting surface.

Watson says that he was certain that Nicklaus would hole the putt, and hole it he did from some forty feet for one of the most extraordinary birdies. The stands erupted, and rarely has the final green at an Open championship witnessed such scenes. Nicklaus, ever the sportsman, urged the crowd to be quiet, to allow Watson to putt, and to his credit he stroked in his putt for victory by a single stroke!

Surely no one who witnessed the scene as the two left the arena, arms around each other, will ever forget it. Watson will be remembered as the winner, but they will both be remembered for an outstanding display of golf and sportsmanship in one of the truly great Opens.

1978

Owen Comes Close to Spoiling Jack's Party – But Not Close Enough!

RIGHT: *Jack Nicklaus pictured in full flow at St Andrews.*

BELOW: *American Ray Floyd birdies the 72nd hole to secure a tie for second position.*

ANY OPEN CHAMPIONSHIP PLAYED at St Andrews is a special one, and this Open of 1978 was no exception. Huge crowds flocked in to see the world's greatest players, and by the close of the third day the attendance record for an entire championship had been broken.

The question on everyone's lips was whether or not Jack Nicklaus could win again. It had been three years since he had won a Major, and some believed he was past his best.

After the first two days 24 players were within four shots of the lead. At the top of the leader board at five under par was Spain's new superstar Seve Ballesteros and two players with totally contrasting putting styles – Isao Aoki from Japan, who putted with a wristy action and the toe of the putter in the air, and Ben Crenshaw, arguably the world's finest putter, who was desperate to win an Open Championship, especially here at St Andrews.

Hard on their heels came the familiar names of Nicklaus, Weiskopf and Kite, and from Japan two less well-known names, Tsuneyuki (Tommy) Nakajima and Norio Osaki. The game of golf continues to thrive in Japan. At each Open more Japanese players appear, and surely one year they will produce the champion.

On the third day a completely unknown New Zealander, Simon Owen, began to make a huge impact on the championship. He was a pre-qualifier, and his opening rounds of 70 and 75 meant little, but a best-of-the-day 67 shot him up the leader board to four under par. Only two other sub-70 rounds were recorded for the day, 69s from Nicklaus and Peter Oosterhuis.

The lead changed hands all afternoon and, as so often happens, the famous Road Hole 17th played its part. Of the 80 players who competed in the third round only 19 achieved par at this hole. There were 47 fives, 11 sixes (including Ballesteros), two sevens, and from Nakajima a disastrous nine. Having been on the green in two, he putted into the treacherous Road Bunker and took a further four strokes to get back on the green. In the circumstances his 76 was not a bad score.

At the end of the day Watson and Oosterhuis shared the lead on 211 (five under par), one ahead of Nicklaus, Owen, Kite, Crenshaw and Aoki – quite a formidable line-up!

Overnight the wind suddenly changed direction and now the players would have it in their faces going out and behind them coming home. It is rumoured that Nicklaus felt this was in his favour and delayed his flight home in order to extend his imminent celebrations!

The first of the leaders to falter was, surprisingly, Watson. It just wasn't his day and he faded out of contention with a 76. Floyd, however, with an inward nine of 31 was round in 68 for a four-round total of 283 (five under par) and led in the clubhouse. He was soon followed in on the same mark by Kite and Crenshaw, who after a poor start birdied the 17th and 18th holes. An enormous putt, the length of the 17th green, meant that he was the only player in the field to break par at this hole for the four rounds, with three pars and this birdie.

Oosterhuis had his chance to join this group, but three putts on the 17th cost him dear and he was out of it. So the destiny of the championship lay in the hands of the three Americans already in the clubhouse and Nicklaus and Owen in the penultimate pair.

After a poor start Owen suddenly came alive with three birdies around the Loop at the far end of the course to be five under par, but with a birdie at the 12th to match Owen's, Nicklaus led by one. When Owen birdied the 14th and chipped in at the 15th for another, the championship looked to have turned in his favour again, but Nicklaus still looked calm and in control and he played the 16th perfectly. His second shot was hit to some eight feet and in went the birdie putt. Owen meanwhile had been slightly unfortunate with his second that skipped through the green, and he needed three more to get down. His one-stroke lead had turned in minutes to a one-stroke deficit. Nicklaus was now in the driving seat, and with immaculate pars on the closing two holes the championship was his. Owen sadly took five at the Road Hole and finished tied second with Crenshaw, Floyd and Kite. But his had been a wonderful performance for a qualifier and he put up another fine showing the following year at Royal Lytham.

Nicklaus had defied the critics, and in winning here became only the fourth man in history to win the Open twice at St Andrews. Moreover, the others being Braid, J.H.Taylor and Bob Martin, he was and still is the only one to do so in the 'modern era'.

ABOVE: *Many doubted if Nicklaus would ever win another Major championship but in 1978 he proved that he was far from finished.*

RAYMOND FLOYD

*R*AY FLOYD WILL *always be remembered as a truly great golfer, but the Open title is the one of the four Major championships to have eluded him. A regular and popular visitor he came close on several occasions but it was Jack Nicklaus in particular, in 1978, who foiled his bid to join the illustrious group to have won all four Major titles. However, a US Masters and US Open title, two US PGAs plus a host of other wins in the United States have been some consolation.*

CHRISY O'CONNOR SR

*T*HERE CAN BE *few stronger candidates than Christy O' Connor for the title of the finest player never to win the Open. Blessed with both rhythmn and grace, he finished in the top five on six occasions, twice just behind Peter Thomson and just behind Arnold Palmer in 1961. As well as many tournament wins including the World (Canada Cup) in 1958 O'Connor also played in the Ryder Cup an impressive ten times, creating a then new record.*

Ballesteros Ignores Fairways to Take First Open!

1979

BELOW: *The Spanish sensation Seve Ballesteros holes yet another birdie putt on his way to a first Open success. A six on the 17th ruined Ben Crenshaw's chances.*

THE CHAMPIONSHIP RETURNED to Royal Lytham and St Annes on the Lancashire coast. Five years earlier, when Gary Player won, he had been the only man to break par for the four rounds. This was the case again, only the champion being under par – testament to the quality of the course. It was running fast this year, with a north-westerly wind all week.

For once Jack Nicklaus was not the favourite. That honour went to Tom Watson, who had been winning tournaments and many dollars in the States but had not won a Major since his classic confrontation with Nicklaus at Turnberry two summers ago. Others tipped as the prospective champion were Hale Irwin, who had just won his second US Open (being a straight hitter is an advantage at Lytham in particular), Ben Crenshaw and Seve Ballesteros, although many felt that his wildness off the tee would be his undoing.

1979

As happens so often, an unknown name stole the limelight on the first day, and this year it was Scotsman Bill Longmuir. Out in 29, home in 36, his 65 was the lowest round of the day by three strokes. But almost predictably he fell away with rounds of 74, 77 and 82 to finish tied for 30th place on 298. However, not many people can claim to have played nine holes in the Open Championship in 29!

On the second day it was the turn of Ballesteros to bring the course to its knees. His 65 was made on the last five punishing holes, all par fours that the Spaniard played in four under par. This left him alone in second place, two behind Irwin, who had put together two immaculate 68s. Not far behind lay the big names of Watson, Nicklaus, Crenshaw and Aoki.

For the third round, played in deteriorating weather with blustery conditions, Irwin and Ballesteros were paired together at the back of the field. Despite hitting the ball much straighter, Irwin just could not shake off the Spaniard, and his frustration was visible as time and again Ballesteros would get up and down from bunkers or make the green from seemingly impossible positions. This was not a style of golf that Irwin was used to! In difficult conditions they both took 75 and so there was no change at the top of the leader board. But Nicklaus had crept closer following a 73, as had Crenshaw, Aoki and Mark James after a second consecutive 69. Australian Rodger Davis, who would become a regular competitor in the championship, and a popular one at that, had put himself in the hunt with consecutive 70s to be just four strokes off the lead.

After just three holes on the final day Irwin's lead had gone and he was one behind Ballesteros. The Spaniard had started 2, 4, 4 to Irwin's 3, 4, 6 and his challenge was effectively over. A disappointing 78 saw him finish in sixth place on 289.

As so often happens towards the end of a Major championship the name of Nicklaus began to creep up the leader board, and with a fine birdie at the 16th he moved to two over par, which was how he would finish – on 286. The championship now lay between him, Ballesteros and Crenshaw, although Davis had gone to the turn in 32 and led for a while (6, 5, 6 on the 14th, 15th and 16th would be his undoing). Mark James too had put up a fine performance, finishing on 287.

With just a few holes to play, Crenshaw seemed favourite, as he had covered most of the dangerous holes whereas Ballesteros had not, but not for the first time

BEN CRENSHAW

*W*HEN CRENSHAW ARRIVED *on the scene as a professional he was the most talked-of player since Jack Nicklaus. An avid believer in the traditions and history of the game, Crenshaw has had the Open as his ultimate target for many years. Second twice and with a string of top ten finishes, some say that he tries too hard to win this title, thereby doing himself no good. Probably blessed with the finest putting stroke of his generation, Crenshaw has gained some consolation with two Masters titles.*

1979

LEFT: *Ben Crenshaw has two Masters titles to his name but the championship he most wants to win, the Open, has eluded him by the closest of margins on several occasions.*

at Lytham the 17th proved crucial. When he walked away from the hole with a six his hopes were dashed. The sight of Crenshaw, a man passionate about the history of this championship and desperate to win it, leaving the clubhouse later with tears of despair and disappointment in his eyes is one that will linger a long time.

And so the destiny of the Open lay in the hands of the 22-year-old Spaniard. Despite blasting the ball to all parts of the course he somehow kept saving par and even made birdies. At the 12th he got down in two from a horrible spot and at the 13th he holed from off the green for a birdie. At the 14th he finally succumbed to par, but again at the 15th he got down in two having missed the green. He clinched his victory on the next hole after missing the fairway by some 30 yards. Having taken a free drop he hit a wedge to 15 feet and holed the putt for his birdie. A potential five or six had become a three, but that is the way Ballesteros plays the game. Pars followed on the final two holes, so having missed the last seven fairways he had still played these holes in one under par!

Some said that Ballesteros was a lucky champion, but his skill around the greens was magical. At the age of 22 years and 3 months he became the youngest Open Champion this century and brought a new breath of excitement and dash to the game – of which we would be enjoying much more for years to come.

1980 *Watson in a Class of His Own*

~

FOLLOWING HIS VICTORY at Royal Lytham the previous summer Seve Ballesteros had gone on to become the youngest ever winner of the Masters at Augusta in April (winning by four strokes having been ten ahead with just nine holes to play). Now Jack Nicklaus had returned to form and confounded all his critics by winning the US Open at Baltusrol just a few weeks before.

And so the scene was set for the Open Championship. The venue was Muirfield and the favourites for the title other than Ballesteros and Nicklaus were Trevino (enjoying a good spell after a slump), Watson and Crenshaw.

For the first time in its history the championship was scheduled to finish on a Sunday. Golf was following the example of many sports that had begun to use both days of the weekend. These were, after all, the two days of the week that the general public could watch sport, whether live or on television.

Although the first day saw dull weather, with a cloudburst at one point, some fine scores were produced. Jack Newton, who had come so close at Carnoustie in 1975 and had just come second to Ballesteros at Augusta, returned a 69. So too did Nick Faldo, one of the up and coming young British stars. However, at

LEFT: *A young Nick Faldo practises with Jack Nicklaus and Tom Watson at Muirfield in 1980. Between all three of these great champions they have won an impressive total of 32 Major titles and 11 Opens.*

1980

LEFT: *A jubilant Tom Watson salutes the crowds on his way to glory at Muirfield. A superb third round 64 spreadeagled the field and ultimately he was champion by four strokes from Lee Trevino.*

the end of the day the familiar names of Trevino and Watson were at the top of the leader board following rounds of 68.

Trevino continued his fine form on the second day with a 67 to give him a three-stroke advantage over Watson, Ken Brown of Scotland and Jerry Pate, a previous US Open Champion. Just a further two strokes away were the dangerous names of Newton, Ballesteros and, from the United States, Nicklaus, Crenshaw, Andy Bean and Dr Gill Morgan. But the round of the day belonged to Argentinian Horatio Carbonetti. His 64 was a wonderful round, but sadly it came after a 78 – and another followed on the third day, which was one too many to make the cut for the final round.

On Saturday, the third day, both Brown and Crenshaw returned 68s to keep well in the hunt. Isao Aoki shot a staggering 63, made up of nine threes and nine fours, to equal the championship record, but his round was still not the most important of the day. Tom Watson went to the turn in 34 but with a stunning homeward nine of 30 he spreadeagled the field and opened up a four-stroke lead. Quite simply, he made the game look easy and this was as near to perfect golf as is possible.

Watson gave his opponents little chance on the Sunday, and with birdies on the 7th, 8th, 9th, 11th and 12th, victory was his. Round in 69 for a total of 271, this was the second lowest 72-hole total in Open history (his own 268 at Turnberry in 1977 being the record!).

With gallant last rounds of 69, Trevino, Crenshaw, Britain's Carl Mason and Nicklaus finished next, in that order. Another name to note at the finish was that of American Bill Rogers. Having only made the cut on the qualifying score of 149, he finished with rounds of 68 and 69. More would be heard of him at Royal St George's the following year.

This was a superb exhibition of clinical golf from Watson, and his third victory in the Open Championship confirmed him as the world's leading player at the time.

1981 *Rogers Putts to Victory at Sandwich*

BELOW: Bernhard Langer's Open career has seen him twice finish runner-up and three times third but to date the ultimate prize has eluded him. At Royal St George's in 1981 his four round total of 280 gave him outright second place to the Texan Bill Rogers.

Aᴏғᴛᴇʀ ᴀ ɢᴀᴘ ᴏғ 32 ʏᴇᴀʀs the championship returned to the south-east corner of England, to Royal St George's at Sandwich. The Open had previously outgrown Sandwich, but new roads had been built and now the R&A took courage in their hands and brought the championship back to this much-loved course. There is no doubting the quality of the course. It has many wonderful holes and the finish is one of the toughest in the land.

Tom Watson started a very short-priced favourite but never quite got going, and disappointing last rounds of 75 and 73 saw him in a tie for 23rd place. It is rare that a disastrous round is the main headline in the newspapers, but that is what happened after the first day. Despite a brave finish of 3, 3, 5, 4 against a par of 4, 3, 4, 4 Jack Nicklaus took 83 strokes, his highest ever score as a professional. Admittedly he played in atrocious conditions and his compatriot Craig Stadler took the same score. The following day they responded magnificently, Nicklaus taking 66 and Stadler 68, but sadly Stadler's score of 151 was one too many to proceed to the weekend.

1981

LEFT: *Third placed Raymond Floyd and Open Champion Bill Rogers deep in conversation preceeding the presentation ceremony.*

On the first day, hardly surprisingly, no one broke the par of 70 and only England's Nick Job and Argentinian Vicente Fernandez matched it.

Scoring conditions were considerably easier on the second day and Nicklaus's 66 was matched by Bill Rogers, a prolific dollar winner on the US circuit. He had just come second to David Graham in the US Open and was the reigning World Matchplay Champion, but for some reason had not been seen as a potential winner here. Rogers' total of 138 gave him a single-stroke advantage over Ben Crenshaw (67), still seeking that elusive Open title, and Nick Job. Close on their heels were Bernhard Langer (one of only three professionals in Germany but already making quite an impression in Europe), Watson, Jacklin (making a welcome return to form), Mark James and David Graham.

A third-round 76 sadly spoilt Crenshaw's chance and by the end of the day there were realistically only three possible winners: Rogers, whose fine 67 put him at five under par, and Langer and Mark James, both on level par.

Surely with such a lead Rogers would follow his second place in the US Open with victory here. But by the time he had holed out for a double bogey seven at the 7th his lead was down to one over Langer and two from Floyd, who had made a late charge for the title. But birdies at the 9th, 10th, and 12th averted the crisis and Rogers was safe once again. When he reached the 18th tee he had four strokes in hand and his only remaining problem was getting past a policeman who did not recognize him!

It is ironic that it was Rogers' friend and fellow Texan, Ben Crenshaw, who had been instrumental in persuading him to travel over in pursuit of the title Crenshaw himself craved so much. After just two attempts Rogers was taking the title home!

Rogers returned just twice more, finishing 8th in 1982, and in the US Open that year he finished a fine third to Watson, but thereafter he gradually disappeared from the top of the golfing rankings. His golf, in particular his putting, had been of the highest quality at Sandwich and there was no doubt he was a worthy and popular champion.

Sandwich itself was voted a great success, and the R&A took the unusual step of taking the championship back there just four years later.

1982

First Two Rounds to Clampett, but It's Watson after Four

BELOW: *Opening rounds of 67 and 66 gave young American Bobby Clampett a huge lead but then a 78 and 77 saw him slip to joint 10th place, four strokes behind Tom Watson.*

ALTHOUGH BOBBY CLAMPETT did not win the 1982 Open Championship, his name will always be associated with it. At Royal Troon (the club had received its Royal Charter in its Centenary year of 1978) the young American led the field by five strokes after two rounds of 67 and 66. Although only 22 at the time, he was 20th on the US Tour money list and had just come third in the US Open. After five holes of the third round he led by seven, but then it all fell apart and he finished in 77 and 78 to tie for tenth place with Jack Nicklaus.

Under perfect skies, Clampett, playing links golf in the British Isles for the first time, led after two days from Nick Price, at the time a relatively unknown Zimbabwean but who would have much say in future Major championships around the world. Just two strokes further back lay the menacing name of Watson and also that of Scotland's Sandy Lyle, who had previously played in the event as a 16-year-old.

Fine weather continued for the third day, but a stiffening wind made the back nine, one of the fiercest in golf, a proper test. Only three players broke par in the day – Faldo, Trevino and Japan's Masahiro Kuramato. Clampett, playing with Price in the final group, made a shaky start, but birdies at the 4th and 5th (both par fives) steadied the ship and at this point he was seven strokes clear of his nearest rival, Irishman Des Smyth.

Then disaster struck on the 6th, at 577 yards the longest hole in championship golf in the British Isles. Clampett visited three bunkers on this one hole and walked away with an eight to Price's par five. To his credit he played reasonable golf for the remainder of the round, dropping only four shots when under the severest of pressure, but sadly there were no birdies to balance the books.

Of the main challengers only Faldo and Kuramato managed to break par with 71s, but despite this the field had bunched up so that the leader board going into the final round looked like this: 211 Clampett. 212 Price. 213 Smyth, Lyle. 214 Tom Watson. 215 Kuramato, Oosterhuis. 217 Faldo, Denis Watson, Zoeller.

The first significant move made on the final day was by Faldo, who birdied the 1st and eagled the 4th on his way to a fine 69 and a two-under-par total of 286 that set a target for the last three groups. A short while later Oosterhuis made a wonderful birdie on the final hole to edge past him and set a new target of 285.

Out on the course Tom Watson had made a huge move by eagling the par-five 11th Railway Hole, courtesy of a perfect three-iron to just a yard. This took him to five under par and a share of the lead with Price. Watson then dropped a stroke at the 15th, but par golf home saw him in on 284, one ahead of Oosterhuis and leader in the clubhouse.

The destiny of the championship now lay in the hands of Price who, having birdied the 10th, 11th and 12th, had a three-stroke lead with six holes to play. A three-stroke lead may seem quite a cushion, but anyone who has seen the last, few holes of a Major championship knows the pressure these players are under. Price, at the time, was relatively inexperienced in the Majors and the next hour or so was to cause him much pain.

A stroke went at the 13th, and at the 15th, a tough par four, he took six when he hit his second into a bunker he claimed to be unaware of and only just got out. In the space of three holes his lead had disappeared. A par followed at the 16th but another stroke went at the notoriously tough long par-three 17th. All of a sudden the Championship had slid from his grasp and he now required a birdie on the final hole to tie Watson. After a hooked tee shot he played a fine second to the back of the green, but sadly the putt to tie pulled up short.

So, just three weeks after stealing the US Open from Nicklaus at Pebble Beach by chipping in at the 71st, Watson was champion for a fourth time, and was honest enough to describe his victory as follows: 'I didn't win this championship – I had it given to me.'

Price, to his credit, took defeat with great dignity. His time would come, but not before more pain, this time at the hands of Ballesteros. So ended a wonderful championship, played in front of huge crowds in glorious sunshine.

ABOVE: *All smiles from Tom Watson having fought back from two behind Nick Price over the closing holes to capture his fourth Open title in eight years.*

PETER OOSTERHUIS

*B*ORN IN LONDON *in 1948, Oosterhuis has the unique record of being selected for the Walker Cup while still at school! A fine professional career followed, with a third place in the Masters in 1973 (having led by three strokes entering the final round), and he was second in the Open to Gary Player in 1974 and to Tom Watson in 1982 – no mean achievement.*

BERNHARD LANGER

*H*AVING TURNED PROFESSIONAL *in 1972 aged only 15, Bernhard Langer became one of Germany's few golf professionals and its first truly successful one. His Open career first took off in 1981 wehn he finished second behind Bill Rogers at Royal St George's and in 1984 he was to finish second again, this time behind Ballesteros at St Andrews. Three third places have also been achieved but the ultimate prize has so far eluded him.*

1983

It Doesn't Get Much Better than This. Ask Tom!

I F THE 1982 CHAMPIONSHIP had seemed an exciting one, the following one at Royal Birkdale was even more so.

Despite a lean time at home in the regular tour events Tom Watson had motivated himself sufficiently for the Masters, where he finished tied for fourth place behind Ballesteros, and for the US Open, where he lost by a single stroke to Larry Nelson. And so he arrived as favourite to take a fifth Open title.

On examining the course many felt it had been set up unfairly, the wet spring and hot early summer having resulted in the severest of rough. Some thought the greens perfect – the best they had seen in an Open Championship – while others, Watson included, felt they were too soft and not in the mould of classic links greens.

Whatever they all felt, some stunning scores were produced. Despite starting 6,6, Faldo returned an excellent 68, helped by a 3,3 finish against the par of 5,4. Watson produced a 67, Bill Rogers likewise, his score helped along by the rarest of birds, an albatross two on the par-five 17th after holing a one-iron second shot!

But the round of the day belonged to the American, Craig Stadler. When he got to eight under par after 16 holes, the lowest ever score in the Open looked a real possibility. In the end he failed to make a birdie four on the 17th, a stroke went at the final hole too, and he had to settle for a 64!

Not everyone achieved wonderful scores, however. Take two of the leading players in the previous championship, Bobby Clampett and Nick Price. After his disappointing end to the 1982 Open and just one hole here at Birkdale, Clampett must have felt that this was an event he was destined never to win. He needed eight strokes to hole out and under the circumstances his eventual 74 was not a bad score. Price meanwhile took nine at the 13th and Denis Watson, the South African who had done so well the previous year, took ten at the 10th!

If the first day belonged to Stadler, then the second belonged to a completely unknown player. Denis Durnian, a club professional from Manchester, played the first nine holes with three pars and six birdies – 28 strokes and he even missed from ten feet on the 9th for a 27! This was the lowest nine-hole score ever in any of the four Major championships. To his credit he kept his game relatively under control and was home in 38 for a 66. A 74 followed the next day, but a fine 67 was recorded on the last day to give him a total of 280 and joint eighth place – a fantastic achievement! When he left Manchester at the beginning of the week, only in his wildest dreams could he have imagined this!

Stadler's second-day 70 kept him just ahead of the field, but there were many big names looming not far away – Trevino (making a welcome return to form), Watson, after a 67 and a 68, Faldo, after two 68s, Irwin, Rogers, Floyd, Langer, Graham Marsh and Hal Sutton, who would go on to win the US PGA the following month.

The quality of the golf was reflected in the cut-off after 36 holes. At 146 it was the lowest in the history of the championship, although 12 years later at St Andrews it was 143, one under par!

Starting the third round just one stroke behind Stadler, Watson made just the start he did not want – a six on the 1st. However, he settled down, made eight consecutive pars and was home in 70 for a three-round total of 205. At the end of the day this was good enough to leave him in the lead. A strong wind had made scoring conditions for the leaders more severe and any score of par or better was a fine one. A host of players were still in a position to take the title and the leader board looked like this: 205 Watson. 206 Stadler. 207 Graham, Faldo, Floyd. 208 Trevino. 209 Irwin, Mark McNulty, Andy Bean, Fuzzy Zoeller. 212 Ballesteros, Bill Rogers. Even the last two still had an outside chance.

So, to the final day: Faldo flattered early on and at one point led, but a poor back nine left him tied for eighth place. Graham, Stadler and Floyd all disappointed and faded away with 75s. It was the globetrotting Graham Marsh, brother of the Australian wicket-keeper, who took the championship by storm. Starting his final round some three hours before the last group and eight strokes off the lead, he put together a score of 64 for a total of 277 that saw him in the clubhouse in a very strong position. With the wind picking up, his total began to look better and better! But when the giant American Andy Bean and his compatriot Hale Irwin holed out in the penultimate group, both with 67s, Marsh's dream was over. Now they led by a single stroke and the only person out on the course who could better them was Watson.

Watson had seen the score that Marsh had posted and he knew what Bean and Irwin were up to ahead. A first nine of two-over-par 36 was not that encouraging, but Watson then started to play the sort of golf that only true champions play when the pressure is on.

RIGHT: *Despite last round charges by Graham Marsh (64), Andy Bean (67) and Hale Irwin (67), Tom Watson prevailed by a single stroke to join James Braid, J.H. Taylor and Peter Thomson as a five times winner.*

1983

RIGHT: *Amidst excited, cheering crowds and having just played a majestic two iron to the final green, Tom Watson's Open victory is just moments away.*

A birdie putt went in at the 11th, and at the par-five 13th he picked up another stroke. On the short 14th a six-foot putt for par with quite a break went down. A par followed at the 15th, and at the 16th he holed from five or six yards for another birdie. Standing on the 17th tee he needed two pars to win, and with the par-five 17th reachable in two it seemed a real possibility. But a hooked tee shot into the dunes, reminiscent of Trevino twelve years earlier, gave him no chance of reaching the green and he settled for a par five.

In the previous three rounds Watson had missed the fairway on the 18th and now he was faced with needing a par on one of the toughest par fours in golf to win the Open. His response was to rifle a drive miles down the middle of the fairway, leaving himself 218 yards to the pin. He then played, under the utmost pressure, one of the greatest shots possible to win a Major championship. With the crowd arguably let in slightly too close, a waggle or two of the two-iron followed, and then he let rip with the most perfectly balanced swing. With a touch of draw the ball settled some 20 feet from the hole and the championship was his. Should anyone ever doubt that Tom Watson was a *great* champion, his play over the last nine holes and that two-iron to the final green should change their minds!

This was a wonderful Open, containing some sensational golf. Many, including Denis Durnian, will never forget it! Nor will Hale Irwin, who finished only one stroke behind Watson. At the 14th on the third day he was just three inches from the hole and he casually stroked at the ball with the back of his putter – only to have an air shot!

Watson's fifth title put him alongside champions such as Braid, Taylor and Thomson and only one behind Vardon.

THE ERA OF BALLESTEROS, NORMAN AND FALDO

1984-1993

WITH THE INCREASE IN COMPETITION from all over the world the championship has become harder for one person to dominate in recent times. However, in this ten-year period there is no doubting that Severiano Ballesteros, Greg Norman and Nick Faldo were the leading figures, sharing seven championships between them. In their victories they have produced some of the lowest scoring ever seen in the event's history, golf of the highest quality and always drama and excitement.

Ballesteros's wins at St Andrews in 1984 and at Lytham in 1988 saw the Spaniard at his magical best. In 1986 at Turnberry Greg Norman finally turned the corner and destroyed the opposition, and at Royal St George's in 1993 he produced possibly the finest last round ever to see off the world's best.

Nick Faldo's three wins proved to himself and the golfing world the value of his utter dedication, and that the rebuilding of his swing was worthwhile, for over a five-year period he was without doubt the world's leading player.

RIGHT: *The perfect setting: glorious sunshine and huge crowds surround Nick Faldo on the final green at St Andrews as he completes a five stroke victory over Mark McNulty and Payne Stewart.*

1984

Ballesteros Denies Watson Sixth Title

AS EVER, ENORMOUS CROWDS FLOCKED to St Andrews for another spellbinding championship that was in doubt right to the end. A record 193,000 people attended – 50,000 more than ever before – for the first time ticket sales exceeded one million pounds, and for the third year running there was fine weather!

Scotsman Bill Longmuir, who at Lytham in 1979 had started with a 65, was up to his old tricks and started with a best-of-the-day 67, only matched by Greg Norman and Peter Jacobsen. At the other end of the scale disaster befell 1981 champion Bill Rogers, who took a seven-over-par 12 on the 14th!

On the second day, again played in wonderful weather, Longmuir kept up his fine play only to spoil it all with a seven on the treacherous Road Hole 17th. He finished with a 71 for a six-under-par total of 138, but this was four more than that of an unknown 23-year-old Australian, Ian Baker-Finch. He had produced rounds of 68 and 66 and with his easy-going manner and long, willowy swing he looked to be thoroughly enjoying himself. At ten under par he led by three shots from Trevino, Ballesteros and Faldo – but surely he could not withstand the pressure?

On the third day, however, to confound the sceptics Baker-Finch holed a huge birdie putt on the 1st green and promptly went out in 33 to be 13 under par! With the homeward nine playing into a slight wind he took 38 for a 71 and an 11-under-par total. Matching him at 11 under was none other than Tom Watson, who had produced one of the rounds of his life, a seven-birdie, six-under-par 66. Just two further behind were Ballesteros and Langer with fine rounds of 70 and 68 respectively. The championship seemed destined to go

RIGHT: *Seve Ballesteros celebrates victory with the Claret Jug outside the 'home of golf'.*

LEFT: *Maybe...maybe...yes! Yes! Yes! Seve Ballesteros, the Spanish maestro, birdies the 72nd hole to secure victory over Bernhard Langer and Tom Watson in another scintillating Open championship.*

to one of these four as there was a further five-stroke gap to the next challengers. Surely Sunday, 22 July was the day that Tom Watson would equal Harry Vardon's record of six Open Championships.

With fine last-round scores of 68 and 69 respectively Fred Couples, playing in his first Open, and fellow American Lanny Wadkins set the target at 281, seven under par. Of the penultimate pair, Ballesteros and Langer, it was the Spaniard who was always just ahead. As they prepared to play the 17th he stood at 11 under par, with the German nine under.

Just behind in the final pairing were Watson and Baker-Finch. The unfortunate Australian's woe had started as early as the first hole when his pitch shot spun back into the Swilcan Burn. His challenge was effectively over after just a few holes and he would finish in 79 despite bravely holing on the final green for a three.

So could Watson do it? He appeared to be in control, but at the 12th strangely used his driver from the tee, which seemed unnecessary, and ended up in a bush. A penalty drop was required and a crucial stroke was dropped. For the first time in a week Ballesteros made a par four on the 17th and strode to the 18th. Watson, back on the 17th tee at 11 under and level with Ballesteros, flirted with danger and his drive ended on the right side of the fairway. He seemed unsure what club to play but finally hit a two-iron, compared with the six-iron Ballesteros had played. His ball flew the green and landed beyond, stopping just two feet from the wall. From there he could not make a par and as he walked off to the last hole the crowds ahead erupted as Ballesteros holed a birdie putt from some 15 feet.

Suddenly Watson had fallen two behind and needed a two on the last to tie, which was too much to ask into the wind. With a par four and a ten-under-par total of 278 he shared second place with Bernhard Langer. Ballesteros was champion for the second time and Watson's chance of a sixth title had gone. He will rue his choice of club on the 17th for a long time!

1985

Scottish Glory As Sandy Scrapes Home

∽

ABOVE: *Twice US Open champion and once US PGA champion, the flamboyantly dressed Payne Stewart was always a popular visitor to the Open where he was twice runner-up.*

Following the successful restoration of Royal St George's to the Open rota in 1981, the championship returned to Sandwich just four years later. The extent to which scores at a links course are determined by the wind can be gauged by comparing the three championships hosted here in the 1980s and 1990s. In 1981 only Bill Rogers broke par for the four rounds. In this year's championship of 1985 no one broke par, and Sandwich is not the longest of the courses used. In 1993, however, when there was wonderful sunshine and no wind, the four-round championship record was broken by Greg Norman with 267, which was 15 strokes lower than this year's score and 13 below par.

Despite a blustery wind on the first day there were some fine scores but none better than Christy O'Connor Jr's 64, a superb effort in the conditions. This left him four clear of a group of four players that included Scotland's Sandy Lyle and David Graham of Australia.

Tougher weather on the second day produced higher scores and only Irishman Eamonn Darcy and Bernhard Langer managed to break par. Rounds of 71 from Lyle and Graham left them leading, with a cluster of players nearby, but many of the big names had suffered in the conditions.

On the third day Lyle and Graham went out together in the final pair and Graham immediately birdied the first hole and was soon two strokes ahead. In the middle of the afternoon a thunderstorm suspended play for a while, but when it cleared the crowds were treated to a late afternoon of glorious sunshine and to Concorde coming straight down the 18th fairway at low level!

Lyle struggled to a 73, but fine 68s from Graham and Langer left them tied at the top of the leader board with one round to play, with Lyle two behind them. Graham's round could have been even better, for it included three putts at both the 16th and 17th.

Sunday dawned with real hope of a British victory or at least a European one, with Langer, Lyle, Woosnam and O'Connor all on the leader board. Early in the day a fine par round of 70 and a nine-over-par total of 289 saw the young Spaniard José Maria Olazabal in as the leading amateur, and it would not be many more years before greater things were to come from him.

The early leader was another Spaniard, José Rivero, whose fine last-day 68 set the target at four-over-par 284. In the afternoon it was still anyone's game as three or four over par still looked a possible winning score. But soon Rivero's score was beaten when a young American, Payne Stewart, finished with a fine 68.

1985

LEFT: *Lyle falls to his knees in despair as he fails to chip out of Duncan's Hollow on the final green. Despite this he secured a bogey five and scraped home by a single stroke from Payne Stewart.*

Then Tom Kite suddenly came into the picture and looked a possible winner. After 62 holes he led the championship, but a six at the 10th proved his undoing and he would end three strokes too many. With four or five holes remaining the outcome lay in the hands of Stewart, Graham, Lyle, O'Connor and Langer.

It was Lyle, playing with O'Connor, who set a new target of 282. A huge putt went down at the 14th and another followed at the 15th for a birdie. Suddenly he was in the lead and this was still the case when he stood on the 18th tee. Two fine shots saw him just off the putting surface on the left side of the green in a slightly grassy lie. A delicate chip was required, through Duncan's Hollow, up the slope to the pin on the other side of a ridge. His chip never had quite enough strength, and as his ball rolled back almost to his feet Lyle fell to the ground in despair.

A fine putt followed but his ball agonizingly rolled three feet past. O'Connor then holed out to great acclaim from the crowd and sportingly appealed for quiet for Lyle. Sandy stroked the ball into the hole, and there followed a strange sense of relief that he had avoided taking six but also disappointment at his dropping a stroke.

By now only Langer or Graham could prevent the first British win since Tony Jacklin's in 1969, or the first Scottish win since Tommy Armour's at Carnoustie way back in 1931 (although Armour was domiciled in the USA). But for the second day running the last three holes were Graham's undoing. Dropped shots at the 15th, 16th and 18th left him two strokes more than Lyle's total. With Lyle watching from behind the final green, Langer needed a birdie to tie. Just over the back in two, he played a wonderful chip that actually hit the hole but ran on four feet past. Sadly he missed the return putt to tie Stewart for second – a highly expensive miss.

So, a Scottish victory at last! Wonderful scenes ensued as the crowd lapped up a home win that proved to be a catalyst for a golden period of European success in the Majors and the Ryder Cup.

Although everyone was happy for Lyle, David Graham will always feel that he let slip a great chance of victory. This was the closest he would ever get to holding the Claret Jug.

1986

Norman, at Last

~

FOLLOWING THE UNFORGETTABLE 1977 open duel between Watson and Nicklaus, Turnberry was again the host club in 1986.

The weather on the first three days of this championship can be summed up in one word – vile. With strong winds and rain, par of 70 on the first day was a fine score and only Ian Woosnam of Wales could match it. There was much complaining by many of the leading players about the severity of the course. In places the fairways were just 20 yards wide, with rough like jungle. Nicklaus, the Masters champion, Floyd, the US Open Champion, and Lyle, the holder, were all blown away and each took 78.

One person not complaining was Greg Norman. On the second day, following a first-round 74, he equalled the all-time championship record score of 63, which

BELOW: *The 9th tee at Turnberry – one of golf's greatest settings but a terrifying challenge in poor conditions.*

RIGHT: *In contrast to later days, Greg Norman drives from the 9th Bruce's Castle in glorious weather conditions with the famous Turnberry lighthouse seen in the background.*

included three-putting the 18th. Admittedly by now the greens had softened up considerably and the wind was not so severe, but his score was achieved under far tougher conditions than Mark Hayes's 63 here in 1977 or Isao Aoki's at Muirfield in 1980. This remarkable round left him on 137, three under par and two ahead of England's Gordon J. Brand and four ahead of Nick Faldo and Japan's leading player, Tommy Nakajima.

Further bad weather, possibly worse in fact, drenched players and spectators alike on the third day, and a 74 left Norman now just one ahead of Nakajima, who had bravely finished with two fours for a fine 71. Two strokes further back were Brand (75) and Woosnam, whose fine 70 matched the lowest score of the day.

On Sunday, 20 July the weather finally relented, the sun shone and the question on everyone's lips was: 'Can Greg Norman finally win a Major?' After all, he had come so close many times before and this year had led going into the final round of both the Masters and the US Open.

Having started with rounds of 76 and 75, Seve Ballesteros had only just survived the halfway cut. A third-round 73 was a little better but on this final day, starting out very early at 14 over par, he produced a closing round of 64 that was to leave him tied for sixth place. He would finish ahead of Nakajima who went out in the last pairing! He then sadly three-putted the first from five feet and faded away with a 77.

The question everyone was asking of Norman was answered early in his final round when he holed a bunker shot on the 3rd for a birdie that put him five strokes clear of his pursuers. Despite fine efforts from Brand (71), Langer (68) and Faldo (70), he was never seriously challenged and over the closing holes he marched his way to victory. His 69 gave him a par-equalling four-round total of 280, all the more extraordinary in that it included a 63!

Finally, after so many disappointments, Norman had won his first Major championship, and his victory was a hugely popular one. A charismatic, dashing player, he is a huge crowd puller and one of the true superstars of the modern game. His achievements are all the more extraordinary in that he only took up the game at the age of 17.

BELOW: *Greg Norman whose charisma and sporting flair made him one of golf's great favourites with the crowd.*

1987

Eighteen Straight Pars Give Faldo First Victory

ABOVE: *Mintues earlier Paul Azinger, a young American on his first visit to Scotland, looked like the winner all over, but a 6, 5 finish let in Nick Faldo for his first title.*

THE CHAMPIONSHIP RETURNED to Muirfield on the east coast of Scotland, arguably the finest links course in Great Britain and one of the finest in the world.

The world's leading players were present, including the past four champions to have won at Muirfield – Player, Nicklaus, Trevino and Watson. Also challenging for the title was the American Paul Azinger, the season's leading money winner on the US Tour, who was playing links golf in the British Isles for the first time.

The first day belonged to Australian Rodger Davis with a 64. Out early, he took advantage of the best conditions with a wonderful round containing eight birdies. As the day went on the wind increased and it became colder and colder, and under such conditions Nick Faldo's 68 was a fine score. However, other fine rounds were recorded, notably 67s from the American trio of Ken Green, Trevino and Bob Tway. There were also 68s returned by Azinger, Nick Price and Larry Mize, who had just won the Masters after an outrageous pitch into the hole to deny Greg Norman another Major title.

On the second day, when steady drizzle fell all day, another 68 gave Azinger a single-stroke lead from Faldo, Davis, Gerard Taylor, another Australian, who had to qualify, and Payne Stewart. A further stroke behind were Tom Watson, Craig Stadler, the South African David Frost and Bernhard Langer, but sadly he faded away the following day.

On the third day the weather was even worse. A driving north-easterly wind made conditions thoroughly unpleasant for players and spectators alike, and some high scores were recorded. Ballesteros took 77, Player 79 and Nicklaus 81. Although several 70s were returned it was thought that Lyle's 71, in the worst of the weather, was the round of the day.

Taylor, the qualifier, shared the lead for a while at six under par, but almost predictably faded away and his last two rounds were 75. However, 25th place overall was a fine performance.

The leader board see-sawed, with Frost, Faldo and Azinger all at the head of affairs at some stage, but at the end of a long and cold day it read: 207 Azinger. 208 Faldo and Frost, 209 Watson, Stewart, Stadler. So for a second time Tom Watson was in a great position to challenge for a sixth title to match Harry Vardon's record.

The final day saw the sea mist, or haar as it is known locally, shroud the course for much of the day, giving the impression that it was November not July! Azinger, out with Frost in the final group, seemed to have the title in his pocket after an outward nine of 34 in which he holed everything asked of him. However, strokes went at the 10th and 11th, and ahead of him Stewart was making a challenge after an eagle three at the 9th to go to five under par.

Davis, after a disappointing 74 the previous day, strung together a run of birdies in the middle of his round. This was followed with a birdie four at the 17th, and a brave up and down from the island bunker on the final hole saw him in with a 69 to set the target at 280.

While the hopes of Watson, Stadler and Frost did not come to fruition, Faldo was stringing together par after par. However, when Azinger reached the 17th tee he still led by one and was still favourite to win. A good drive at this par five makes a birdie a real possibility, but Azinger's drive finished in a deep fairway bunker and six was the best he could do.

Playing ahead was Faldo, who had just recorded his 17th consecutive par thanks to some wonderful recovery shots from greenside bunkers. Not looking at scoreboards but just concentrating on his own game, Faldo then played two perfect shots up the final hole to the front of the green. His approach putt ran some three and a half feet past the hole, leaving him a horrible downhill putt back, but to his and the crowd's relief it fell in for a remarkable 18th consecutive par and a total of 279.

Immediately the stands erupted as the leader board showed Azinger had taken six, and so now he needed a par at the final hole to tie Faldo.

A fine drive left him in a good position, but his approach shot to the green was dragged into a bunker from which he could not get down in two.

And so in the space of minutes this championship had changed completely. Faldo's relentless determination for perfection and three years of intense work under the scrutiny of his coach David Leadbetter had finally paid off. The next five years would see him as the dominant figure in world golf.

LEFT: *Popular American visitor Craig Stadler looks on as Faldo plays to the short 16th. A series of 18 consecutive pars by Faldo secured him the title from Paul Azinger and the Australian competitor Rodger Davis.*

1987

1988 — *More Magic from Seve*

THE CHAMPIONSHIP RETURNED to Royal Lytham and St Annes for the first time since Ballesteros's swashbuckling victory of 1979. But the Spaniard had not won a Major since the 1984 Open and few thought he could regain the magic to win again.

To defy the doubters he started the championship with three birdies! Five under par after ten holes, he finished in 67 to lead at the end of the day, and this was achieved in wet and windy weather – a great round of golf.

Much-improved weather followed on the second day and the players out early made the most of the conditions. Ballesteros, however, was out later in the worst weather of the day, and his 71 was an excellent score in the conditions. But his total of 138 was only good enough for second place at the halfway stage, for

RIGHT: *Seve Ballesteros' brilliant chip shot to the 72nd green at Royal Lytham finishes inches away thereby ensuring his third Open triumph.*

LEFT: *Seve Ballesteros displays his boldness, flair and dash as a player to the full. His last round duel with Nick Price produced golf of the highest quality.*

Nick Price had followed up his opening 70 with a brilliant 67. Faldo was on 140, with a host of the world's top players not far behind.

Yet again there was a change of weather on the Saturday, and following a deluge of rain play was abandoned for the day. So, for the first time in 128 years, the championship would finish on a Monday.

When the third round was finally completed there appeared to be just four players who could realistically win. Price led on 206, followed by Ballesteros and Faldo on 208, and Lyle on 209. Only Fred Couples, with two eagles on the front nine, threatened these four, but his challenge was to fade over the closing holes.

On the last day, with Faldo, Ballesteros and Price playing in the final group, birdie followed birdie. The first important turning-point came at the 7th, which Price and Ballesteros both eagled to Faldo's par, following an unlucky bounce. Lyle's challenge had faded and suddenly it looked like a two-horse race.

Both men continued to play flawless golf and, despite four birdies from Ballesteros to follow his eagle, Price refused to yield. At the 12th the Spaniard dropped a stroke but promptly birdied the 13th, as did Price, whose second shot finished just three inches from the hole! Ballesteros replied at the 16th by hitting his nine-iron to just a few inches, and by now a matchplay feel between the two had evolved.

After both players had made par fours on the 17th Ballesteros led by one stroke, and on the final hole the Spanish wizard conjured up another magical chip from the edge of the green, lipping the hole and ending just inches away from it. Price, with a putt of some thirty feet to tie, charged it past and then missed the return, and so Ballesteros had won his third Open title and his second at Lytham.

For the first time in years he had looked completely at ease and happy with himself, and his closing 65 will go down as one of the great last rounds to win a Major championship.

After coming so close at Troon in 1982, and here scoring 69 when leading by two strokes and still not winning, poor Nick Price must have wandered just what he had to do to take this title. However, when Ballesteros played golf as he had this week there was no one in the world to match him for excitement and theatre.

1989

Calcavecchia Takes First Ever Three-Way Play-Off

THE WORLD'S LEADING PLAYERS, including twelve past champions, assembled at Royal Troon to compete for the 1989 championship. For the first time in five years there was fine weather, with temperatures in the high eighties, and with the course bone dry there was some spectacular scoring.

As happens so often a complete outsider led early on, and this year it was the Australian Wayne Stephens. His six-under-par 66 gave him a two-stroke advantage

BELOW: *From left to right: Norman, Grady and Calcavecchia pose for the press before the first three way play-off in the event's history.*

1989

over the Americans Couples and Azinger, the Spaniards Martin and Olazabal, Romero of Argentina and fellow Australian Wayne Grady, who two weeks earlier had won his first event on the US Tour.

Stephens held on gamely on the second day with a level par 72, but at the end of the day it was his compatriot Grady who led, having added a 67 to his 68. Two behind was the formidable pair of Tom Watson and, after a course record 65, Payne Stewart, still seeking this title having finished 2nd, 4th and 7th in earlier years. Lurking just four from the lead lay the menacing names of Greg Norman, Fred Couples and Mark Calcavecchia, the American player who had finished runner-up to Sandy Lyle in the previous year's Masters.

Another day of wonderful weather greeted the players for the third day and apart from Romero, who took 75, all the leading players were under par for the day. Grady held on to his lead, but only by the smallest of margins. After another 68 Watson was on his heels and again in a wonderful position to equal Harry Vardon's record. Stewart, Couples, Calcavecchia and the easy-going Irishman David Feherty were all within three strokes of Grady.

Before starting his final round Greg Norman had predicted that he would need a 63 to have a chance of victory, and he promptly started with six consecutive birdies! At 11 under par he was right in the thick of things, and when he completed his round some two and a half hours before the leaders, his 64 for a 13-under-par total of 275 had set quite a target. Grady, meanwhile, had birdied two of the first five holes to go 15 under par and continued to lead.

Calcavecchia, playing two groups behind, looked as if he was just beginning to fade. But on the 11th he holed a huge putt to save his par and on the 12th, when in a seemingly impossible position short and left of the green (with little of it to play with), he lobbed his pitch shot straight into the hole full toss for a birdie! When he hit his second shot on the final hole to four feet and holed for another birdie he had tied with Norman!

1989

BELOW: *Calcavecchia is the new champion having completed the four hole play-off in two under par.*

Meanwhile neither Stewart nor Couples could break the par of 72 and their challenge petered out. Watson, having started so well (with a birdie at the 1st), began to miss crucial short putts, an affliction that had crept into his game in recent years, and he finished two shots too many. Grady, in the last group, stood on the 71st tee needing two pars to be Open Champion. How his putt from twenty feet for par on the 17th stayed out he will never know, but on the 18th he secured a solid par four and so for the first time in 118 Open Championships there was to be a three-way play-off.

The R&A had, in their wisdom, brought in the system of a play-off over four holes, thereby ensuring that the championship would be decided on the same day, a good decision for players and spectators alike.

Norman continued from where he had left off earlier and birdied the first two holes. However, at the treacherous 17th Calcavecchia was the only one of the trio to make a par three and he and Norman went to the final hole level, with Grady seemingly out of it, two behind. Calcavecchia hit a slightly poor tee shot into the right rough and then Norman pulled out his driver and hit an enormous drive. With the adrenalin flowing he hadn't considered that he could reach a fairway bunker 310 yards away – but he did.

When Calcavecchia hit a superb five-iron to six feet the pressure was really on Norman. Up against the face of the bunker he blasted at the ball, only to reach another bunker, and when his next shot flew over the green and out of bounds Mark Calcavecchia was Open Champion for 1989.

Having correctly predicted what was required earlier in the day and having then got himself into such a wonderful position, Norman must have rued his choice of club on the final tee, for this was the third occasion he had lost in a Major play-off, but that is the type of player he is – aggressive and exciting.

However, Calcavecchia's performance was no surprise as he had already won twice on the American tour earlier in the year and was in a rich vein of form. Grady, meanwhile, gained some revenge by winning his only Major when he took the US PGA title the following year at the Shoal Creek Country Club in Alabama.

FRED COUPLES

A REGULAR VISITOR to the Open, Couples has to date finished in the top ten on seven occasions, but victory at Augusta in 1992 in the Masters remains his only Major success. Capable of sensational bursts of scoring, particularly in the last round, Couples is blessed with an elegant, easy-looking swing and there would be few more popular winners of the championship than he.

PAYNE STEWART

W HEN PAYNE STEWART appeared in the early 1980s he made quite an impact with the quality of his play and his colourful clothing. In 1985 he finished just a single stroke behind Sandy Lyle at Royal St George's and in 1990 he was second again at St Andrews. He also won two US Open titles in 1991 and 1999. Tragically just months after his second US Open triumph he was killed in an aircraft disaster. This popular man is greatly missed by all in the game.

Faldo Untouchable

1990

S<small>T ANDREWS OPENS</small> always seem to have an extra touch of magic and this was the case again in 1990 for the 119th Open Championship.

Following a successful defence of his Masters title and third place in the US Open Nick Faldo understandably started as favourite.

For the second year running the weather was glorious and scoring was extremely low, the 36-hole cut-off being 143, which was one under par, the lowest ever. Poor Arnold Palmer, at the age of 60, was level par for the two rounds but did not survive to the weekend!

On the first day Faldo signed off a wonderful round by holing his run-up second at the 18th for a two to be in on 67. But Greg Norman, vying with Faldo at the time to be number one in the world, went one better with a 66, matched by his fellow countryman Michael Allen. Rounds of 68 were returned by Sam Torrance and Martin Poxon of Britain, Peter Jacobsen, a popular and regular visitor from

B<small>ELOW</small>: *Nick Faldo drives from the 18th tee at the end of his third round 67.*

1990

America, and the Australians Craig Parry and Ian Baker-Finch, back at St Andrews after his last-round disappointment in 1984.

The second day seemed a repeat of the previous one – perfect weather and low scoring. Norman carded another 66, aided by a full pitch shot on the 14th spinning back into the hole for an eagle three, while unknown Briton Jamie Spence added a 65 to his opening 72. Faldo continued to play immaculate golf, peppering the flag at hole after hole with his approach shots and inevitably holing the putt. He matched Spence's 65 and at halfway shared the lead with Norman on 132, equalling Henry Cotton's record set as far back as 1934.

And so the stage was set for the 'dream' pairing on the third day, with Faldo and Norman going out together in the final group. Meanwhile other players were setting the course alight. Paul Broadhurst in only his second year as a professional followed up opening scores of 74 and 69 by going out in 29 and completing the round in 63 to equal the all-time Open record. Baker-Finch too was out in 29 and home in 35, and his 64 for a 12-under-par total of 204 left him well positioned.

Faldo, however, made his intentions clear at the very first hole when he rolled in a birdie putt to take the lead. After eight holes there was little in it but then suddenly everything went wrong for Norman with three putts on the 9th, 10th and 12th greens. Faldo meanwhile had birdied the 9th and 11th and in the space of a few holes was four ahead. Norman's woes continued with dropped strokes at the 13th, 15th and 16th resulting in a disastrous 76 to Faldo's 67 (that gave him a three-round Open record score of 199). Surely this sudden nine-stroke swing haunted Norman for years to come, and never more so than at Augusta on the final day in 1996.

To his credit Norman bounced back with a 69 on the final day to tie for 6th, but with one round to play Faldo led by five strokes from Payne Stewart (68, 68, 68) and Baker-Finch, with both Parry and Broadhurst one and two strokes further back respectively.

With the sort of golf he had displayed all week, Faldo was not the man to give away a five-stroke lead, and for the second day running he started in determined fashion, hitting his second shot stiff at the opening hole. At the 4th a stroke was dropped after he was bunkered for the very first time in the championship – a remarkable feat in itself when one considers how the Old Course is littered with them.

Meanwhile up ahead the Zimbabwean Mark McNulty, a regular visitor to the championship, shot up the leader board with a closing 65 to go 13 under par and lead in the clubhouse on 275.

Only Stewart of the other challengers appeared to have any chance of spoiling Faldo's march to glory, and after a string of birdies around the turn he got to within two of the leader. But that was as close as he came, for he dropped a stroke at the 13th and when Faldo hit a magnificent iron to six feet at the 15th the championship was effectively over.

His last-round 71 for a total of 270 gave him victory by five strokes. His rivals had been left in his wake by a devastating display of golf that confirmed him as the leading player in the world at the time.

BELOW: *By winning his second Masters and Open titles, 1990 was undoubtedly Nick Faldo's year. At St Andrews he displayed his brilliance by finishing the week 18 under par and five strokes clear of his rivals.*

1992

LEFT: *The dramatic closing scenes of the 1992 Open at Muirfield as seen from the air.*

This last-day 73 gave him a four-round total of 272, victory by one from Cook and two over Olazabal, whose 68 took him ahead of Pate by one. More importantly, it was his third Open title and he became only the second player, along with James Braid (1901 and 1906), to win it twice at Muirfield.

Faldo had, as he had demanded of himself, played the best and bravest four holes of his life at just the right time.

1993

Norman's Record-Breaking Championship

ABOVE: *Norman powers away his second to the 71st hole and victory is just minutes away.*

FOR THE THIRD TIME in 13 years and the twelfth in all, Royal St George's at Sandwich staged the championship. Arguably the strongest ever field for the Open assembled at this magnificent and popular venue.

Like all links courses, Sandwich on a windy day is a severe test of golf, but this year the course had been slowed down by rain just beforehand and during the championship itself there was little wind. Over the years there have been many classic head-to-head finishes, such as the one at Turnberry in 1977, but rarely have so many of the world's top players been in contention for the championship over the last 18 holes.

After pleasant weather in practice, the first day was damp but calm and ideal for low scoring, as was shown by the fact that 38 of the field scored under the par of 70. After a poor start Greg Norman, so well liked by the British crowds, birdied five of the last six holes for a 66 and a share of the lead with fellow Australian Peter Senior and the Americans Fuzzy Zoeller and Corey Pavin.

The second day was another day for low scoring and belonged to the defending champion Nick Faldo who, with seven birdies and no dropped shots, equalled the lowest championship round of 63. His play was quite immaculate and the day ended with him one stroke ahead of the popular Bernhard Langer (66, 68), Norman (66, 68), Pavin (66, 68) and Fred Couples.

After a third day of yet more low scoring (Wayne Grady of Australia posting 64) the leader board saw Pavin and Faldo sharing the lead on eight under par with Norman and Langer one stroke behind.

The first of these four to slip away on the final day was Pavin, whose par round of 70 was not enough to keep him in contention. The remaining three vied for the lead with never more than one stroke separating them until the 9th, where Norman, with his fourth birdie of the round, found himself two strokes ahead. But Faldo and Langer kept attacking him with birdie after birdie. Langer's only lapse was at the par-five 14th, the Suez Canal hole. Using his driver on the hole for the first time in the week, he cut his drive out of bounds into the ditch that runs perilously close to the fairway the entire length of the hole and the result was a title-wrecking seven. Much to his credit he immediately birdied the next two holes and finished in 67 for 270, a total that would have won any previous Open in history, excluding 1977.

Hard as he tried, Faldo could not quite close the gap on Norman. Even with a slight lapse at the 17th, where he missed from no more than two feet, the Australian marched down the 18th to huge applause, and after an immaculate closing four the championship was his by two strokes from Faldo. His last round of 64 must be considered as one of the greatest fourth rounds in championship history.

This was a marvellous Open with many records torn to shreds. Norman's total of 267 beat Tom Watson's record of 1977 by a stroke. The young South African prodigy Ernie Els became the first man in Open history to break 70 in each round – Norman achieved this later in the day of course – and the Amateur Champion Ian Pyman set a new record for an amateur in the championship of 281.

For many people, however, the abiding memory at this great sporting feast was the sight, at the presentation ceremony, of 91-year-old Gene Sarazen, who had won the Open 61 years ago at the adjoining Princes Golf Club, in discussion with Norman. To see the warmth and mutual respect shown between these two champions was a great moment in golfing history.

1993

BELOW: *An historic meeting as the 91-year-old Open champion of 61 years ago, Gene Sarazen, greets the new champion, Greg Norman.*

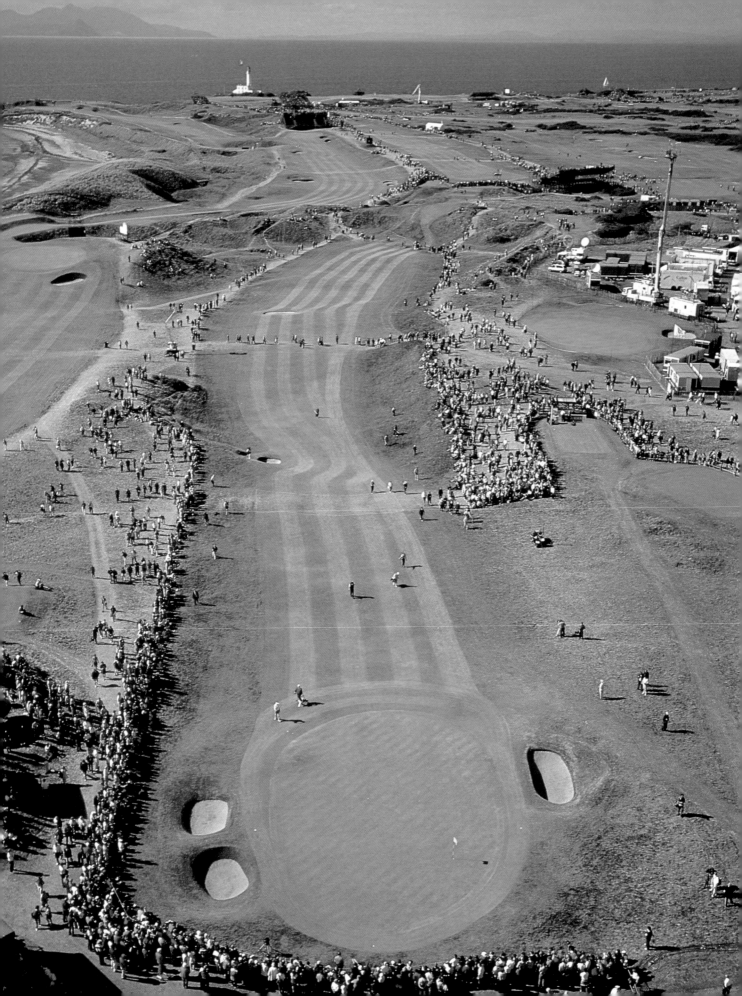

A NEW GENERATION
TAKES OVER
1994–2000

Iᴺ ᴛʜɪꜱ ᴘᴇʀɪᴏᴅ there was no dominant individual. Although the title was won by an American for four consecutive years, it was always by a different one. These years have seen golf of the highest quality, the kind of drama and excitement that we have come to expect from this great event, and the sportsmanship that golf continues to demonstrate.

It will be fascinating to see how the next few years evolve. Will Tiger Woods or Sergio Garcia fulfil their dreams and stamp their authority on the event? Or, as the game continues to grow globally, will we see – as has almost happened but not quite – a champion from Scandinavia, Italy or the Far East?

Lᴇꜰᴛ: *Turnberry is one of the game's most stunning settings. With the Isle of Arran visible in the background, it is seen in all its glory during the 1994 championship.*

Rɪɢʜᴛ: *Arnold Palmer bids farewell to his adoring fans from the Swilcan bridge.*

171

1994

Price Gets Both Hands on Claret Jug at Last

ABOVE: *Nick Price finally gets his hands on the Claret Jug after his spectacular finish at Turnberry. Having previously suffered at the hands of Watson and Ballesteros, his triumph was a most popular one.*

FOLLOWING THE SUCCESS OF ERNIE ELS in the US Open at Oakmont the world's leading players moved on to Turnberry on the west coast of Scotland. Another week of high drama with an enthralling finish was witnessed by those who travelled to this stunning location.

Following a cold spring with hardly any rain in May or June, the course was saved at the last minute when rain finally came and the sun shone to give growth. The result, miraculously, was a course in superb condition! In true Scottish tradition, after three days of practice with no wind it blew on the first day of the championship. However, many good scores were returned (a 65 from New Zealander Greg Turner being the lowest of the day) although one exception was Faldo, who played the wrong ball out of the rough on the 17th on his way to an eight. He finished in 75 and blamed no one but himself for the incident.

Many fine scores followed on the second day, the best being American Mark Brooks's 64, but it was Tom Watson who led, rolling back the years with rounds of 68 and 65. One behind him was a young Swede, Jesper Parnevik, who had come 21st the previous year, and the American Brad Faxon, one of the world's great putters. One further back was Nick Price, who had come so close to winning before, only to be denied by Watson and Ballesteros.

Turnberry was bathed in sunshine on the third day and more scores were recorded under par than over it! Having only just made the cut, and despite an upset stomach, former Masters Champion Larry Mize shot a 64, as did the American Fuzzy Zoeller. Price returned a 67 to stay firmly in contention, but with one day to go at least ten players were still in a position to win.

Again fine weather was the order of the day and both Faldo and Swede Anders Forsbrand scored 64s to climb into the top ten. With nine holes to play there were many still in with a chance. Sadly, the first to make a backward move was Tom Watson, whose short putting let him down again, and a subsequent 74 left him well down the field.

It was the Swede, Parnevik, following ten consecutive pars, who made the first forward move with birdies at the 11th, 12th, 13th, 16th and 17th! His putting was simply brilliant. Only Price could stay close to him, and to do so he had to play remarkable golf. On the 14th, however, his second shot bounced some 30 yards through the green leaving him with a tricky bump and run shot from the barest of lies. Price played the shot of a lifetime to three and a half feet, holed the putt and he was still alive!

When Parnevik walked to the final tee, however, for a moment he had a three-stroke lead and surely the championship was his. Here he made his only mistake, going for the pin with his second shot rather than the heart of the green. His ball fell away left and short and he took three more to get down. But he was round in 67 for a total of 269 and he still led by two.

Just behind, Price kept his hopes alive by making a birdie on the 16th and then at the 17th holed surely one of the most extraordinary putts ever seen in this championship at such a crucial stage. Some forty feet away in two, he faced a nasty curling downhill putt, but somehow it fell in for an eagle. Price leapt feet into the air – in the space of minutes he had come from three behind to one in front. Needing a par four at the last he made no mistake and played the hole immaculately.

At last Nick Price was Open Champion! – he had wanted this championship so much after his previous disappointments – while Parnevik was left to reflect on what might have been. Price attributed much of his success to his loyal caddie of many years 'Squeaky' Medlin, who tragically two years later would succumb to leukemia.

Price went on to win the US PGA by six strokes the following month for a second time and ended the year as the outstanding player in the world. There is no finer example of a true sportsman than he.

ABOVE: *Nick Price drives from the 9th tee with the majestic granite rock of Ailsa Craig visible in the background.*

1995

Rocca Magic but Big John Takes the Title

Following ben crenshaw's emotion-charged victory in the Masters and Corey Pavin's first Major success in the US Open, St Andrews was the venue for the 124th Open Championship.

Huge crowds were treated to another totally absorbing and dramatic championship, played in increasingly tricky wind conditions.

The favourites for the title struggled: Nick Price, the defending champion, was out of sorts and Nick Faldo started with a 74.

Tom Watson was so disappointed the previous year at Turnberry, having been in a great position to emulate Harry Vardon's six wins only to fade over the last few holes. He was back at St Andrews to try again and made a great start with a five-under-par 67. His score was matched by the controversial, long-hitting John Daly, who had made golfing headlines in 1991 when winning the US PGA title. Daly had only managed to enter the event at that time through another's withdrawal and he had not even had time for a practice round. Also on 67 was Crenshaw, still pursuing the elusive Open title that he wanted to win so much, especially at St Andrews.

The second day saw tremendous performances from two great past champions, Gary Player and Jack Nicklaus. Both made the halfway cut, Nicklaus doing so despite taking ten on the 14th in his first round, having taken several shots in Hell Bunker. Another fine performance came from the 6 foot 8 inch Scottish amateur, Gordon Sherry. Fine rounds of 70 and 71 seemed to confirm his great potential, but sadly it has not as yet come to fruition.

Faldo, following his 74, came roaring back with a 67 but that was the best he would achieve in the week and his challenge faded away. His fine score was matched by the Americans Brad Faxon and John Cook and theirs were the lowest scores of the day.

But the abiding memory of this second day was Arnold Palmer's emotional walk over the Swilcan Bridge and up the 18th fairway for the final time. The fact that many other players were there, past champions included, shows the extent to which he is revered.

At halfway it was anyone's guess as to who would win with a leader board looking like this: 138 Daly, Faxon, Tomori; 139 Rocca, Cook, Pavin, Brooks, Els; 140 Singh, Stewart.

One name not on the leader board was that of 25-year-old New Zealand Maori Michael Campbell, but 24 hours later, following a best of the week score of 65,

Above: *Costantino Rocco falls to his knees after holing a 60 feet putt through the Valley of Sin to secure a play-off against John Daly. Like the finals of 1970, 1977 and 1999, this has to be one of the most dramatic finishes to an Open Championship.*

his name was at the top of it! By the end of the third day Campbell had a host of challengers within four strokes of him, but sadly Crenshaw's hopes had been blown away with a 76 and the chance of winning the ultimate prize had gone for another year.

The first significant move on the final day, which was extremely windy, was that of a young Englishman, Steven Bottomley, whose 69 was the best round of the day. Suddenly he found himself leading in the clubhouse, having started the day at just two under par. Soon he was joined by the American Mark Brooks, but of the leaders it was Daly who made the best start with three birdies in the first eight holes.

The Japanese player, Katsuyoshi Tomori, was literally blown away and took 78, Campbell dropped strokes at the 5th and 6th to ultimately tie with Bottomley and Brooks, but still a marvellous performance.

With seven holes to play, Daly already had one hand on the Claret Jug with only the Italian Costantino Rocca seemingly able to catch him. Rocca, the most engaging and popular of characters, had been a regular on the European Tour for some years and had appeared in the Ryder Cup, but could an Italian really win the Open?!

On the 16th Daly took five to Rocca's birdie three and he dropped another stroke to par at the 17th to leave the outcome uncertain again, but a par on the final hole saw him home in one stroke less than Bottomley, Brooks and ultimately Campbell. In the final pair Rocca put his second at the 17th on the road but under the most severe pressure putted up the bank and, needing to hole the putt to have any chance, bravely did so from four feet.

So the Italian stood on the final tee requiring a birdie three to tie, and with a gale blowing downwind the green was just about driveable. A fine drive saw him just short and to the left of the green with a little pitch shot facing him. To his and the entire crowd's dismay he completely fluffed his shot and was left 60 feet from the hole at the bottom of The Valley of Sin.

Rocca looked distraught but he still had one chance left. With Daly looking on he chose to putt, hit the ball firmly and miraculously it ran up the hill and dropped straight into the hole! In seconds Rocca's despair had turned to joy and he fell to the grass thumping the ground with his fists! Surely this was *the* miracle shot in Open history.

And so for the second occasion in the championship's history a four-hole play-off took place and understandably, after the drama of the last half-hour, it was something of an anti-climax. After Rocca dropped a stroke at the 1st and Daly birdied the 2nd it was effectively all over.

John Daly was Open Champion, and as for Rocca, once he had made it into the play-off it didn't seem to matter that he lost – although he probably would not agree! Everyone just seemed to be so happy for him after his seemingly disastrous chip.

Unfortunately John Daly's marital and alcohol problems continued and to date this hugely talented young man has not rediscovered the form that won him the most dramatic of victories at the 'Home of Golf'.

1995

BELOW: *John Daly celebrates as he birdies the second hole of the play-off. Minutes later the title was his when Rocca's ball ended in the notorious Road bunker.*

1996

Lehman Brilliant for Three Days and Just Hangs On

∾

ROYAL LYTHAM WAS THE VENUE for the 1996 Open Championship, eight years after Ballesteros's dramatic win over Nick Price, and 70 years after Bobby Jones's famous triumph. Remarkably, in the seven subsequent Opens at Lytham no American had managed to emulate the great man and take the title. The way the event had grown, meanwhile, can be seen by comparing the attendance figures. In 1926 (the first year gate money was charged) 11,000 spectators saw Jones's victory. In 1996 171,000 attended.

In glorious weather on the first day a host of sub-70 scores were returned, with no fewer than seven Americans scoring 67. At the end of the day, however, the leader following an excellent 65 was the Englishman Paul Broadhurst, who had won the Silver Medal as leading amateur here in 1988.

The second day saw further low scoring. Irishman Paul McGinley went to the turn in 29, aided by a hole in one at the 9th, and his 65 to go with his opening 69

BELOW: Tom Lehman explodes out of one of the rare bunkers he visited in the championship. A closing 73 saw him just get home by two strokes from South African Ernie Els (67) and American Mark McCumber (66).

gave him a share of the lead, with American Tom Lehman, who had just missed out on the US Open by a single stroke.

Incredibly, just one stroke behind was 56-year-old Jack Nicklaus, together with Ernie Els of South Africa and an up and coming, very talented Swede, Peter Hedblom. After two 68s Faldo was just another stroke away, along with several other 'big' names. Two past champions, however, were notable in missing the halfway cut. Ballesteros had shown none of his old flare that had brought him two championships here, and Ian Baker-Finch, champion just five years earlier, was still being affected by nerves on the big occasion.

Another notable name that did survive the cut and was to end the championship as leading amateur at three under par was the young genius from the United States, Tiger Woods, three times US Amateur Champion. Who can predict how many times his name will go down on the Claret Jug?

The third day, Saturday, was another wonderful day with many scores in the sixties, but to the crowd's disappointment Nicklaus faded from the scene with a 77. An eagle at the 6th and birdies at the 7th and 8th helped Faldo to a third 68, to be on nine under par, but the day belonged to one man, Tom Lehman. Playing precision golf and putting like a demon, he made eight birdies on his way to a 64, a three-round Open record of 198 (beating Faldo's 199 at St Andrews in 1990), and a seemingly unbeatable six-stroke lead.

But the Masters of just three months past immediately came to mind. It was there that Greg Norman also took a six-stroke lead into the last round only to take eleven strokes more than his playing partner and the subsequent winner, Nick Faldo. Here at Lytham on the final day it was Faldo who would be Lehman's partner! And Faldo knows Lytham so well, having won the English Amateur title and having beaten Tom Watson over the same links in the 1977 Ryder Cup.

Out just ahead of him and Lehman was Fred Couples who, as he has done so often, made a last-day charge at the title. Out in 30, he was in sight of Lehman, but sadly he required 41 for the inward nine to finish tied for 7th.

The very first hole was a crucial one for Lehman. Faldo hit his opening tee shot to just eight feet but missed his birdie putt and Lehman bravely holed from four feet for a par. A potential two-stroke swing had been avoided. At the 5th Faldo missed another golden opportunity, and then at the 6th Lehman had a lucky break that probably decided the championship. Deep in bushes off the tee, he somehow blasted the ball out and finally holed from four feet for his par and then watched as Faldo missed from just three feet for his birdie.

Faldo could offer no more. It just wasn't his day and in the end he relinquished second place to Mark McCumber, of the United States, and Ernie Els, who both scored 67s. Els had had a great chance to catch Lehman, only to bunker his tee shot at both the 16th and 18th. Lehman's only error was at the 14th; otherwise he played steady and conservative golf. Having been under huge pressure all day, he finally got home with two strokes to spare, round in 73 for a four-round total of 271.

This will be remembered as an Open played in wonderful weather, with golf of the highest quality, and won by a worthy champion.

1996

ABOVE: *It was in 1996 that America's new young superstar Tiger Woods first made an impact on the Open Championship. Still an amateur, his second day 66 matched Frank Stranahan's 1950 record score for one round.*

1997

Ice-Cool Leonard Putts His Way to Victory

GLORIOUS WEATHER and a course in perfect condition greeted the players to the 126th Open Championship at Royal Troon. Only on the first day, with the wind blowing straight down the first nine holes and with some of the holes coming home out of range, did the players suffer. With sun-baked fairways the ball was travelling huge distances. For example on the 402-yard 7th Tiger Woods drove a greenside bunker and on the par-five 4th he drove in excess of 400 yards. With such advantageous conditions 31 players broke or matched par for the four rounds.

When the halfway cut was made at 147, five over par, this is what the leader board showed: Darren Clarke, the young Irishman, led on 133. Justin Leonard, who had won the US Amateur title in 1992, was on 135. A further stroke back was Jesper Parnevik, the Swede who had come so close down the coast at Turnberry in 1994, while Fred Couples and a young Englishman, David Tapping, were four behind Clarke.

Huge crowds, partly no doubt because of the R&A's new policy of allowing free admission to under-18s, and also because of the fabulous weather, flocked to Troon for the weekend.

Tiger Woods had only just made the halfway cut but still believed he could win, and on the third day he gave the crowds just what they had come to see. Out in 32 (including five birdies), he eagled the 542-yard 16th, which played into the wind, having hit the green with two enormous strokes. A chip in for a birdie at the 17th followed, and with a round of 64 he was right back in the championship. But overall the day belonged to Parnevik, whose second consecutive 66 left him two clear of Clarke, with Couples (aided by a rare eagle two at the 11th) and Leonard five strokes off the lead.

The crowds flocked back on the Sunday hoping to see another charge from 'The Tiger'. After birdies at the 4th and 5th he looked on course to make a real challenge, but the shortest hole in championship golf, the Postage Stamp 8th, put paid to his dreams for another year. A treble bogey six completely ruined his momentum and in the end he faded to a 74 and joint 24th position. But without that six, a seven on the 11th on the first day, and an eight at the 10th on the second day, who knows what might have happened?

The charge that everyone expected came not from Woods but another American, Justin Leonard. With six birdies he went to the turn in 31 which moved him into second place alone, after Clarke had a disastrous shank on to the beach at

the 2nd resulting in a double bogey six. To his credit, however, the Irishman fought back and a closing birdie gave him a round of 71 and joint second place.

As the pressure mounted on Parnevik's slender lead it was he not Leonard who showed signs of cracking. With steely, ruthless eyes and a totally focused mind the American played immaculate golf, holing putt after putt, and when a 35-footer rolled down the 17th green into the hole for a two the title was almost his. With the unfortunate Parnevik missing a short birdie putt on the 16th and then taking four at the 17th, it was all over.

No one could deny Leonard his victory, for a 65 in the closing round of the Open when in a position to win is a rare achievement, and as in 1996 the game could have no finer sportsman as its Open Champion. His victory speech, full of charm, dignity and emotion, on a glorious evening on the west coast of Scotland, with the Island of Arran in the background, left hardly a dry eye in the crowd. This was sporting theatre at its best.

ABOVE: *Justin Leonard proudly holds the Claret Jug following his last round 65, played in glorious conditions at Royal Troon.*

1998

Birkdale and O'Meara at Their Best

THE BIRKDALE COURSE that awaited the players for the 1998 Open was a very different one from that of 1991. Acres of scrub and buckthorn had been cut back and several tees moved slightly, but more importantly all 18 greens had been relaid. The old ones had become spongy and less than links-like. The general impression of the new-look course was extremely favourable.

On a warm and generally calm first day Tiger Woods was out early and immediately made the most of the conditions, going to the turn in 30 and coming home in 35. At the end of the day his 65 had been matched only by fellow American John Huston, a veteran of the US Tour since 1983. On 66, one stroke behind, were Nick Price, Fred Couples and the American Loren Roberts, while a host of players were on 67 and 68. Both Mark O'Meara, the current Masters champion, and Lee Janzen, fresh from his US Open victory, opened their campaigns with 72s.

A record crowd of 43,000 made their way to Birkdale on the second day, but sadly they were treated to a strong south-westerly wind and rain. Late in the afternoon play was suspended for some forty minutes with lightning nearby over the Irish Sea, but once it had cleared a beautiful evening followed. Whereas on the first day the average score had been 72, on this brutal second day it went up to nearly 75, five over par!

LEFT: *Brian Watts, (far left) receives the crowd's rapturous applause following his brilliant last hole bunker shot to secure a play-off with Mark O'Meara (left).*

1998

LEFT: *Jesper Parnevik despairs as a putt slides by. An Open title for this popular Swede would be well deserved having just missed out to Nick Price in 1994 with the title seemingly his and having missed out by only two strokes here.*

The star of the day was a 17-year-old English amateur, Justin Rose, who recorded a 66, a remarkable score under the circumstances. Rose had been a prolific winner as a youngster and in 1997 had become the youngest Walker Cup player in history. His total of 138 left him tied with Woods and Nick Price – a dream come true for a young man who had to qualify to get into the event.

But at the end of the day, when the cut-off was made at four over par 144, the leader, following rounds of 68 and 69, was Brian Watts from America, an unfamiliar name to most but in fact playing in the Open for the sixth time. Rather than try to make a living on the gruelling US Tour, Watts had been playing on the Japanese Tour for many years, and earning many millions of yen on his travels.

Many of the leading American players were just one or two strokes behind, including O'Meara who had a fine second-round 68.

If conditions seemed tough on the second day, the players were in for even worse on Saturday, when the average score for the day was over 77! There were some horrendous scores: Phil Mickleson returned an 85, defending champion Justin Leonard an 82, as did Nick Price. Janzen took 80, and Woods 77. Incredibly, Rose, out in the last group with Watts, led the championship after 12 holes and held on bravely to return a 75, which was not a bad score under the circumstances.

Watts also played well when everyone thought he would fade, and his 73 kept him ahead of the field by two. Blessed with an effortless-looking swing and superb rhythm and timing, he was now seen as a serious contender for the title. With one day to go the leader board read: 210 Watts. 212 Parnevik, Furyk, O'Meara. 213 Rose. 215 Huston, Faxon, Bjorn (of Denmark), Woods.

O'Meara's 72 had been the most significant score of the day, and it was not without controversy. Having started with an awful six, when he stood on the 6th tee he trailed Watts by five shots. At 480 yards the 6th is the toughest hole on the course at which to make a par four. O'Meara hit a driver for his second shot which went way right of the green out of sight, deep into the dunes and bushes. Much debate ensued, and at one point O'Meara returned to where he had played the stroke in order to play another, but at the end of 20 minutes of confusion involving many officials, and after a spectator had picked up his ball, he walked off the hole with a five. There is absolutely no doubt that he played the hole entirely within the rules of golf but, as he admitted himself, he had had a lucky break.

The lowest scores of the final day were 66s from Tiger Woods and Scot Raymond Russell for totals of 280 and 281 respectively. Woods's round was completed in extraordinary fashion: after a chip in at the 17th for a birdie he sank a 30-footer at the closing hole to set a good target for O'Meara and Watts, both behind him on the course, who by now were his only real rivals.

Justin Rose walked up the 18th fairway to the loudest cheers of the week. Some 45 yards short of the hole in two, he went straight at the pin with his pitch shot. The ball landed, ran on and literally with its last roll dropped into the hole! Rose had had the week of his life, and although he did not win the championship, his name and his final stroke as an amateur will long be remembered!

O'Meara played a very solid final round, aided by a fortunate break on the 8th, and his round included three twos. When he holed out for a solid par four on the final green for a 68 he had beaten his compatriot and great friend Woods by a single stroke.

The only group left on the course was Parnevik and Watts. The Swede had played a fine round, but his par-equalling 70 was two too many. After a regulation birdie on the downwind 17th Watts stood on the 18th tee requiring a par four to tie O'Meara. The 18th at Birkdale demands a long and accurate tee shot and then a fine second shot, and with the pressure on it is one of the toughest finishing holes in golf. Watts's tee shot was pulled slightly into light rough and his medium iron to the green was always just short, ending bunkered some 30 yards short of the pin. With a difficult lie and with his right foot out of the bunker, Watts then played the supreme shot when under the utmost pressure. He chopped the ball out, it ran on and stopped no more than a foot from the hole.

His rival O'Meara sitting on the bank at the back of the green and applauding Watts's stroke provided a memorable sight and another example of the true sportsmanship these great players display.

The tap-in putt was a formality, and so for the third time in ten years the Open Championship was to be decided by a play-off. O'Meara took control of it at once by birdying the par-five 15th, and the next two holes were halved in par. At the final hole Watts was again in the bunker short of the green in two, but by now the magic had gone, he took five, and with a solid par four Mark O'Meara was Open Champion.

Having played around the world for 17 years, winning many tournaments but none of the Majors, O'Meara had suddenly won two in a single season, just when he thought his time was running out. It could not have happened to a more deserving player. A hard competitor but fine sportsman, he is, in Brian Watts's words, 'a class act'.

RIGHT: *Mark O'Meara plays to the final green in his play-off with Brian Watts in yet another pulsating finish to an Open Championship.*

Lawrie Takes Title after French Farce

≈

FOR THE FIRST TIME IN 25 YEARS the championship returned to Carnoustie, on the Angus coast, just a few miles across the Tay estuary from St Andrews. It was a spectacular return, for the millions of television viewers and thousands of spectators present surely witnessed one of the most extraordinary finishes to any Major championship.

Carnoustie is a fearsome course, but a decline in the quality of the links and lack of infrastructure to cope with the modern demands of the world's leading golf event had seen it taken off the Open rota.

Much of the credit for Carnoustie's revival, following control being handed over in 1980 from Angus Council to the Links Management Committee, must go to its chairman, the late Jock Calder, and to John Philp, the Head Greenkeeper (previously Walter Woods's understudy across the water at St Andrews).

In 1999 Carnoustie was at its most terrifying and, at 7,361 yards, the longest in Open history. Although the fairways and greens were in perfect condition there were murmurings, however, after the practice days. Some fairways were as narrow as 15 yards in places, and that was often where drives would be landing. After two days the murmurings had become major complaints. Many of the game's leading players had quite simply been blown away by the severity of the course.

The first day had belonged to unknown Australian Rodney Pampling, who made the best of the early conditions to return 71, but incredibly missed the halfway cut after a second-round 86! Also missing for the weekend were defending champion Mark O'Meara, who had an 86, Nick Faldo, whose rounds of 78 and 79 meant that he missed the cut for the first time at the Open in 24 years, and Tom Watson, champion here in 1975, who took 82 and 75. Following victory in the Irish Open and second place at Loch Lomond the previous week, the new Spanish phenomenon Sergio Garcia took 89 and 83 – an amazing 30 over par!

Incredibly, the halfway cut was made at 154, which was 12 over par and unheard of in modern times.

At the halfway stage the name at the top of the leader board was that of a relatively unknown French professional, Jean Van de Velde, who had followed an opening 75 with an extraordinary 68. A stroke behind lay Angel Cabrera of Argentina, a regular on the European tour, with Jesper Parnevik, the colourful Swede with such a good Open record, a further stroke back. Tiger Woods, the favourite, lay menacingly just one stroke behind Parnevik, along with Greg Norman and Patrick Sjoland of Sweden.

ABOVE: *With shoes and socks removed and trousers rolled up, Jean Van de Velde contemplates his next move after a disastrous visit to the Barry Burn when victory had been his for the taking.*

1999

RIGHT: *Paul Lawrie holes for a rare birdie at the 17th hole in his play-off victory over Jean Van de Velde and Justin Leonard at Carnoustie.*

Despite the Frenchman's halfway lead there were few present who would have tipped him to take the title, but aided by a red-hot putter he returned a 70 on the third day to lead by five strokes! (despite Australian Craig Parry returning a 67, the best score of the week). After a par round of 71 the 1997 champion, Justin Leonard, was tied with Parry for second place, with Woods, Scotsman Andrew Coltart and David Frost seven behind the leader. Norman was another stroke away. With such a lead surely the first French win since Arnaud Massy 92 years ago was imminent?

On a pleasant final day scoring conditions were considerably easier and the most significant move was made by local Scotsman Paul Lawrie, a regular Tour player for some years, whose previous finest Open finish had been sixth to Greg Norman in 1993. Out in the eighth last group and aided by six birdies, he returned a 67, which left him at six over par, leading in the clubhouse, but was surely too many for a serious challenge.

Woods, Norman and Frost all failed to mount a challenge, but after the Frenchman had struggled out in 38 to his playing partner Parry's 34 his lead had almost gone. For the Australian, however, disaster was not far away. He took a triple bogey seven at the 12th and a double bogey six at the 17th. Despite holing a bunker shot at the final hole for a birdie it was just too many. Leonard still had a fine chance, but a bogey at the 15th and another at the 18th, after visiting the winding Barry Burn left him tied with Lawrie.

Having negotiated the treacherous 16th and 17th holes safely, Van de Velde stood on the 72nd tee with the title apparently in his pocket. He was three strokes clear, and a six would still be good enough for victory. With the stands ahead packed, he sent his tee shot down the right-hand side, leaving himself 195 yards to the green. A medium iron, short of the burn, a pitch up and two or even three putts would be good enough. But no, to everyone's amazement he pulled out a two-iron, cut the shot way to the right, bounced off the grandstand, off the wall of the burn and back behind the burn into heavy rough.

By now Van de Velde was in serious trouble – and his next shot went into the water! Farcical scenes followed, with the Frenchman removing his shoes and socks to contemplate playing from the water with his ball almost submerged. With the ball sinking further and further, he finally saw sense and took a drop. His next went into a greenside bunker, and after splashing out to seven feet he was left with one putt to tie, minutes earlier having had the championship secure.

To his and the crowd's relief the putt went in, and so for the second time in the championship's history three players would contest a play-off. Surely, one felt, Justin Leonard's experience would prove too much for the other two.

With steady rain now falling they went back to the par-four 15th, and hardly surprisingly the Frenchman was the first to suffer, taking six. A birdie three at the 17th kept him in the hunt, but Lawrie matched his birdie to lead by two playing the final hole. Van de Velde had to play short of the burn with his second, and Leonard, going for broke from way back, was in the water for the second time in an hour.

All Paul Lawrie needed now to be Open Champion was one clean strike, and that was just what he produced. His four-iron stopped just four feet from the hole, and when he holed the putt the scenes were both ecstatic and disbelieving. Having had to qualify, in his wildest dreams he could surely not have imagined at the beginning of the week, that on the Sunday evening he would make the short drive home to Aberdeen with the Open championship trophy on the car-seat next to him.

This was truly a fairy story for Lawrie, but Van de Velde's disaster bears comparison with that of Doug Sanders at St Andrews in 1970. To his credit, however, the Frenchman took it well and returned to playing good golf on the Tour immediately.

Despite much criticism of its severity, overall the return to Carnoustie was seen as a success. As had been predicted at the beginning of the week, however, a course set up like this can produce odd results. With four of the first five finishers having had to qualify, that is exactly what happened.

2000

Tiger on Top of the World!

ABOVE: *Tiger Woods punches the air as the final putt drops.*

THE 129TH OPEN CHAMPIONSHIP was always going to be a particularly special event. Played at St Andrews, the Home of Golf, the Millennium Open was a mouthwatering prospect with everyone asking – can anyone prevent American Tiger Woods from lifting the famous old Claret Jug?

After months if not years of planning both on and off the course, 156 competitors began their challenge on the Old Course which Head Greenkeeper Eddie Adams had prepared to perfection, with fast running fairways and true links conditions. In order to prevent the world's top players destroying the famous old links, a few tees had been moved back resulting in a course measuring 7115 yards. Even the weather conditions which had been depressingly poor finally changed and bright sunshine, real warmth and little wind greeted the players and spectators alike.

On the first day the world's finest golfers took advantage of the perfect golfing weather with 75 of the field match par or better.

Tiger Woods, playing with Nick Price and the US Amateur Champion David Gossett, made a steady start with eight consecutive pars but then suddenly the fireworks started around the loop at the far end of the course and he was soon five under par.

At the end of the day Woods was tied with fellow American Steve Flesch on 67 but a shot behind Ernie Els who completed two near perfect nine holes of 33. Els, fresh from his victory at Loch Lomond the previous week, was the favourite of many to prevent Woods from completing the Grand Slam of victory in all four Major Championships.

On Day Two Phil Mickleson, Jose Coceres, Davis Love III and Tiger Woods recorded 66s and this left Woods three clear of his challengers when play ended. However, Day Two surely belonged to Jack Nicklaus who was bowing out of the Open after some 40 years. No one who witnessed his emotional walk up the final fairway will surely forget it and was it purely coincidental that as Nicklaus walked from the 18th green, Woods stepped on to the 1st tee – the end of one reign and the beginning of a new one?

The outcome no one wanted, apart no doubt from those in the Woods camp, was for him to secure the Championship early on but with a third round 66 including seven birdies, he effectively did just that. With one round to play, the world's number one player had a six-stroke lead over the world's number two player David Duval and also Thomas Bjorn of Denmark. A host of other players were another stroke or two behind but they were surely too far away to make a serious challenge to Woods.

2000

LEFT: *Woods drives off the 18th tee on his way to victory at St Andrews, the Home of Golf.*

Despite the near certainty of the outcome, huge crowds yet again flowed into St Andrews on the final day to watch golf history in the making. For the first hour or so it still looked possible for Duval or Els to make a challenge with the gap at one stage reduced to three shots. However, when Duval took four from the edge of the 12th green, the Claret Jug was effectively Woods' for the taking. As he and Duval stood on the 17th tee, Duval was only intent on finishing in second place but he was about to suffer what can only be called a golfing nightmare. In the Road Bunker in two he emerged four strokes later and left the green with an eight on his card. Within minutes he had fallen from second place to joint 11th place. The Road Hole had cost him much heartbreak and sadness as it had done to so many others in previous Open Championships.

Woods' closing 69 for a total of 269 left him an astonishing eight strokes clear of his rivals and reduced the record books to tatters – it was the lowest score in a St Andrews Open and only the third time the champion has had four rounds under 70. Not since the beginning of the century has the winning margin been eight strokes – J.H. Taylor winning by eight on two occasions and James Braid winning by eight on one occasion. For the record books Ernie Els and Thomas Bjorn shared second place at 11 under par with the Americans Tom Lehman and David Toms a further stroke behind.

When Gene Sarazen completed victory in all four Majors he was 33 years old. Walter Hagen was 41 when he achieved the feat, Jack Nicklaus was 26 and Gary Player was 29. For Tiger Woods to achieve the Grand Slam of golf at the age of 24 years is a staggering achievement and who knows what the future will bring? Always considered an impossibility, victory in all four Majors in one year must now be a very strong possibility.

Although the 2000 Open Championship did not end in a classic 'down to the wire' finish, the thousands of people who flocked to St Andrews on Sunday the 23rd of July along with the millions who watched the event on television around the world, all witnessed golfing history made by one of the world's truly great sportsmen, if not the finest.

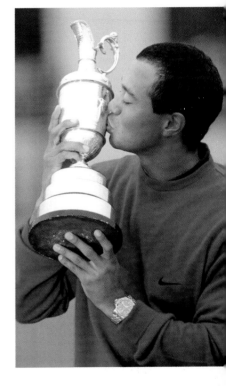

ABOVE: *Victory at St Andrews gave Tiger Woods the Grand Slam of golf victories at the age of just 24 – a remarkable achievement.*

MILESTONES

140 Years of the Open Championship

1860 Willie Park Sr wins the first championship at Prestwick. There are just eight competitors who play three rounds over the 12-hole course.

1867 Tom Morris Sr wins his fourth and final Open at the age of 46 years and 99 days. He remains the oldest player ever to win.

1868 Tom Morris Jr wins his first Open at the age of 17 years and 161 days and in doing so records the first hole in one at in the championship at Prestwick's 8th hole. He remains the youngest player to win any of the Major championships.

1870 Having won the prize, a Moroccan leather belt, three years in succession, Tom Morris Jr is awarded the belt outright.

1871 No competition is held, but Prestwick Golf Club join up with the Royal & Ancient and the Honourable Company of Edinburgh Golfers (then based at Musselburgh) to run the event. From 1872 each club was to host the event in rotation. The new trophy, the Claret Jug that we know today, is purchased for £30.

1872 Tom Morris Jr becomes the first winner of the Claret Jug, at Prestwick – his fourth and final title.

1875 Tom Morris Jr dies on Christmas Day, aged just 24.

1879 St Andrews-born Jamie Anderson wins his third consecutive title.

1882 Bob Ferguson, of Musselburgh, emulates Anderson and wins for the third successive year.

1885 Over 50 competitors challenge for the title for the first time.

1890 John Ball Jr becomes the first amateur and the first Englishman to win.

1892 Another English amateur, Harold Hilton, wins the first Open at Muirfield, played for the first time over two days and 72 holes.

1894 The championship moves to England for the first time, to Royal St George's, Sandwich, Kent. John Henry (J.H.) Taylor wins the first of his five titles and so begins the era of 'The Great Triumvirate'.

1896 Harry Vardon wins the first of his six titles, at Muirfield, after a play-off with Taylor.

1900 J.H. Taylor wins for a third time, at St Andrews, and in doing so has the lowest score in each round – a feat never matched.

1902 Sandy Herd wins his only Open, at Hoylake, using the rubber-core ball recently invented by American Coburn Haskell.

1904 With 144 entrants the championship is extended to three days, at Royal St George's. Jack White wins with 296, the first ever total under 300. He, Taylor and Braid all have sub-70 rounds – the first time this is achieved.

1907 At Hoylake Arnaud Massy becomes the first overseas player to lift the Claret Jug. He remains the only Frenchman to have done so.

1908 Tom Morris Sr dies in St Andrews at the age of 87.

1909 The championship goes to the Royal Cinque Ports Club at Deal, for the first of two occasions. J.H. Taylor wins with a score of 295.

1910 James Braid takes his fifth title in ten years and his second at St Andrews. First prize is £50.

1912 Ted Ray wins his only Open, at Muirfield, and leads in every round for a total of 295.

1914 Harry Vardon wins a record sixth Open, one more than his great rivals Taylor and Braid. The outbreak of war sees the end of their dominance in the game.

1919 The R&A take over the management of the championship.

1920 Deal's second Open is won by George Duncan after two opening rounds of 80 (followed by 71 and 72!).

1922 Walter Hagen becomes the first American to win the championship, at Royal St George's (the first of his four titles in a period of eight years).

1923 Troon hosts its first Open and Arthur Havers beats Hagen for the title by a single stroke.

1925 Jim Barnes, born in England, but a naturalized American, wins the last Open to be played at Prestwick, which has been outgrown by the event.

1926 Regional qualifying and gate money are introduced. The first Open held over the links of Royal Lytham and St Annes is won by the incomparable American amateur, Bobby Jones.

1927 Jones wins again, at St Andrews, and the 290 barrier is broken for the first time, by five strokes!

1929 A second-round 67 helps Hagen to his fourth title, this time at Muirfield.

1930 Bobby Jones wins his third and final championship, at Hoylake, on the way to completing the 'impossible' Grand Slam.

1932 Gene Sarazen wins his only Open, at Princes, adjacent to Royal St Georges, on the only occasion the championship is held there.

1934 Henry Cotton heralds a new era of British dominance by winning at Royal St George's after opening rounds of 67 and 65.

1937 At Carnoustie Cotton beats the entire US Ryder Cup team to take his second title.

1939 Englishman Dick Burton wins the last Open before the Second World War. Sandy Herd plays in his last championship, having first played in 1885!

1946 Following the end of the war Sam Snead wins his only Open, at St Andrews.

1947 Fred Daly becomes the first and as yet only Irishman to take the title.

1948 After a gap of 11 years Cotton wins for a third time, courtesy of a second-round 66 at Muirfield.

1949 South African Bobby Locke wins the first of his four Opens, after a play-off with Harry Bradshaw, following the 'ball in bottle' incident, at Royal St George's.

1950 Bobby Locke successfully defends his title at Troon with a record score of 279.

1951 'Showman' Max Faulkner wins at Royal Portrush in Northern Ireland, the only time the championship has crossed the water.

1952 Locke wins a third title in four years.

1953 Ben Hogan wins on his one and only appearance (at Carnoustie) to become the only person to win three Majors in a season (he didn't play in the fourth). Hogan's first prize is £500.

1954 Peter Thomson becomes the first Australian to win the championship.

1956 Thomson completes a hat-trick of wins, at Hoylake.

1957 The leaders go out last for the final two rounds, and Locke wins the last of his four titles, seen live on television for the first time.

1959 The 23-year-old South African Gary Player wins the first of his three Open titles, all won in different decades.

1960 The Centenary Open at St Andrews is won by Australian Kel Nagle, with Arnold Palmer on his first appearance in the championship just a stroke behind.

1961 Palmer returns to take the first of two successive titles and breathes new life into the championship, encouraging more Americans to enter.

1962 Palmer's second title, at Troon, with a record score of 276 and three of his four rounds in the 60s.

1963 No pre-qualifying for leading players introduced. Bob Charles becomes the first and as yet only New Zealander and only left-hander to win (following the last 36-hole play-off for the title).

1964 'Champagne' Tony Lema wins at his first attempt. Tragically, two years later he is killed in a plane crash.

1965 Peter Thomson wins his fifth title, a record only surpassed by Harry Vardon and matched by Braid, Taylor and subsequently Tom Watson.

1966 Jack Nicklaus wins for the first time and in doing so emulates only Sarazen, Hogan and Player by winning all four Majors. Play extended to four days with Saturday the final day.

1967 Having tried to win for 20 years, Argentinian Roberto de Vicenzo finally does so at Hoylake and is a hugely popular champion. This is Hoylake's last Open, its infrastructure no longer able to cope with the demands of a modern championship.

1968 A 54-hole cut is introduced to the championship. For the first time since official attendance figures were kept, a crowd of over 50,000 witness Gary Player win his second title, at Carnoustie, the longest Open venue.

1969 Tony Jacklin becomes the first British winner for 18 years when he takes the championship at Lytham by two strokes from Bob Charles. Jacklin becomes a national hero.

1970 Having supported the event for several years, American Doug Sanders loses out on the chance of glory when he misses from three feet on the final green at St Andrews. He loses a play-off against Nicklaus the following day by a single stroke.

1971 Three weeks after winning the US Open for a second time Lee Trevino takes the Open title by a single stroke from Taiwan's Liang-Huan Lu, better known as Mr Lu!

1972 Trevino steals the title from under Jacklin's nose after a series of outrageous chip-ins and holed bunker shots. Many say Jacklin never recovered from this ordeal at Muirfield.

1973 Tom Weiskopf wins for the only time, at Troon, having led after all four rounds. A 71 year old Gene Sarazen returns 50 years after failing to qualify in 1923 and holes in one on the Postage Stamp 8th.

1974 The larger 1.68-inch diameter ball becomes obligatory and Gary Player wins his second Open, held at Royal Lytham.

1975 American Tom Watson silences his doubters and wins the first of five Opens after a play-off with Australian Jack Newton at Carnoustie.

1977 For the first time the championship goes to majestic Turnberry on the west coast of Scotland, and Watson overcomes Nicklaus in one of the greatest finishes ever seen. His total of 268 smashes the previous record by eight strokes.

1979 With dashing bravado and flair, 22 year old Severiano Ballesteros becomes the youngest winner of the championship in the century, at Royal Lytham and St Annes.

1980 First scheduled Sunday finish.

1983 Tom Watson wins his fifth Open in nine years, at Royal Birkdale. Complete unknown Denis Durnian scores 28 on the first nine – the lowest score in any Major.

1984 At St Andrews Watson lets slip a great opportunity to equal Harry Vardon's six titles and Ballesteros takes a second title.

1985 Sandy Lyle becomes the first 'true' Scotsman to win the title for 75 years, at Royal St George's.

1986 After three previous runner-up places in Majors, Australian Greg Norman finally fulfils his potential by winning at Turnberry.

1987 With 18 pars in the final round at Muirfield Nick Faldo wins the first of three titles in the space of six years.

1989 At Royal Troon the championship is decided for the first time by way of a four-hole play-off. American Mark Calcavecchia defeats Australians Greg Norman and Wayne Grady after the first three-way tie in 118 Opens.

1990 Record crowds of over 200,000 witness Faldo destroy the opposition at St Andrews and win by five strokes.

1993 For the first time the winner collects a prize of £100,000. Greg Norman is the fortunate recipient at Royal St George's.

1995 At St Andrews, in one of the most dramatic finishes in the championship's history, Italian Costantino Rocca holes a 60-foot putt through the Valley of Sin to force a play-off. However, volatile American John Daly takes the title after the second four-hole play-off.

1996 Tom Lehman's 54-hole record score of 198 enables him to fend off fourth-round challengers and take the title at Royal Lytham.

1999 Scotsman Paul Lawrie starts the day ten strokes off the lead and ends it as Open Champion after a three-way play-off in the first Open at Carnoustie for 24 years. A brutally tough course results in the highest winning score since 1947!

OPEN RECORDS

To produce tables trying to establish who is the finest 'Open player' is unrealistic but fun!

One thing for certain is that Harry Vardon has won more times than anyone else, but does that mean he was a better player than Peter Thomson and Tom Watson, who won less but over half a century later? Certainly when Vardon, Braid and Taylor won their titles there was not the opposition that today's champions face. All they could do at the time was beat anyone else who entered.

For the purpose of this exercise I have produced two separate tables. The first covers the championship from its inception in 1860 to the end of the twentieth century, and the second covers just the twentieth century. However hard I try, it seems impossible to work out a fair method. For example, how fair is it that Young Tom Morris, who finished fourth in 1867 when there were only ten competitors, should score the same points as Nick Faldo for finishing fourth in 1996 from a field of over 150?

However, what can be said for certain is that in the modern era no one has a record in this championship or any of the Majors to compare with Jack Nicklaus. To have won seven more Major championships than any other player speaks for itself. His consistency in the Open was phenomenal between 1963 and 1980, when only twice did he finish outside the first five. Some say that in his heyday his only real competitors were Palmer and Player, and in the United States Billy Casper, but it just was not as simple as that. Vardon, Braid and Taylor had things much more their own way at the turn of the century.

Look at the records of other players as well. Consider how many more Opens Bobby Jones might have won had he not retired at the age of 28! Had war not intervened, would Henry Cotton have secured more than three titles? Many think so.

One can argue for hours as to who was better than who, but all one can be really certain of is who the leading players of their own time were. How can one deny Tom Watson his five victories in just nine years, or Faldo his three in six? With one win compared to Watson's five, how can Sandy Herd achieve a higher ranking? Look at Peter Thomson's record between 1952 and 1958: 2, 2, 1, 1, 1, 2, 1 – it's difficult to find anything to compare apart from James Braid's dominance of the first ten years of the century. It's all hypothetical, but as I have already said, it's fun and quite revealing!

Who knows how these tables will look in one hundred years from now? Will the same names top the tables, or will the stars of today such as Tiger Woods and Sergio Garcia fulfil their promise?

There is one notable name missing from both tables, proving that figures don't tell the whole story. Despite winning the title twice and being hugely responsible for the championship's revival in the early 1960s, the name of Arnold Palmer does not appear, and despite three victories and being possibly the greatest shot manufacturer in the history of the game, Severiano Ballesteros only appears in joint 17th place.

The points system I have used is as follows:
1st 10 points: **2nd** 7 points: **3rd–5th** 5 points: **6th–10th** 4 points: **11th–20th** 2 points: **21st–30th** 1 point

1860-2000		
1.	J.H. Taylor	145
2.	Harry Vardon	135
3.	James Braid	129
4.	Sandy Herd	121
5.	Jack Nicklaus	120
6.	Peter Thomson	112
7.	Old Tom Morris	111
8.	Willie Park Sr	99
9.	Willie Fernie	90
10.	Willie Park Jr	87
11.	Henry Cotton	84
12.	Willie Anderson	83
13.	Nick Faldo	80
14=	Bobby Locke	79
14=	Tom Watson	79
16=	Andrew Kirkaldy	74
16=	Ben Sayers	74
18.	Gary Player	71
19.	Jamie Anderson	64
20.	Young Tom Morris	62

1900-2000		
1	Jack Nicklaus	120
2	Peter Thomson	112
3	J.H. Taylor	109
4	James Braid	108
5	Harry Vardon	86
6	Henry Cotton	84
7	Nick Faldo	80
8=	Bobby Locke	79
8=	Sandy Herd	79
8=	Tom Watson	79
11	Gary Player	71
12=	Lee Trevino	61
12=	Roberto de Vicenzo	61
12=	Greg Norman	61
15=	George Duncan	59
15=	Kel Nagle	59
17=	Walter Hagen	57
17=	Dai Rees	57
17=	Severiano Ballesteros	57
20	Christy O'Connor Sr	56

THE OPEN COURSES

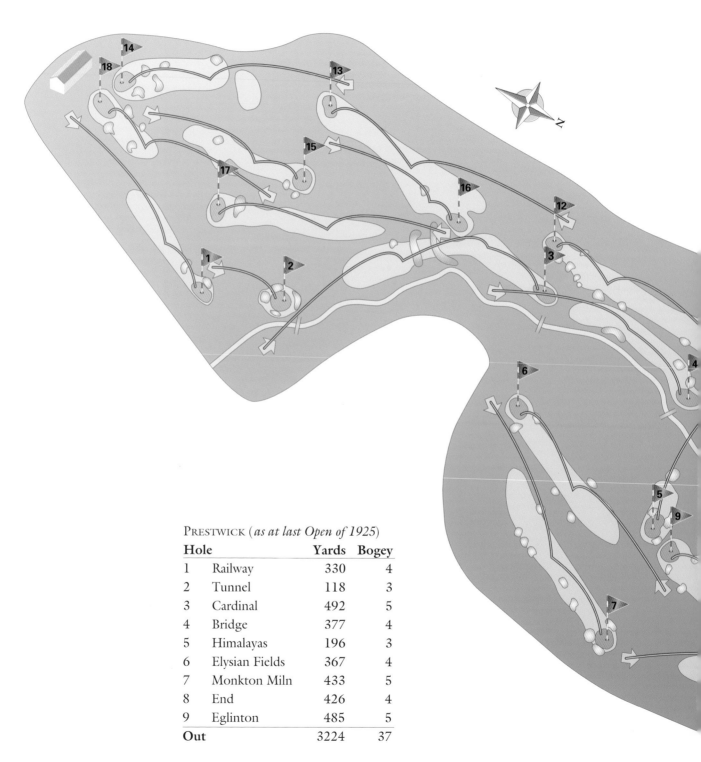

PRESTWICK (*as at last Open of 1925*)

Hole		Yards	Bogey
1	Railway	330	4
2	Tunnel	118	3
3	Cardinal	492	5
4	Bridge	377	4
5	Himalayas	196	3
6	Elysian Fields	367	4
7	Monkton Miln	433	5
8	End	426	4
9	Eglinton	485	5
Out		**3224**	**37**

PRESTWICK

Hole		Yards	Bogey
10	Arran	510	5
11	Carrick	190	3
12	Wall	503	5
13	Sea Headrig	440	5
14	Goosedubs	357	4
15	Narrows	325	4
16	Cardinals Back	233	4
17	Alps	383	4
18	Clock	279	4
In		**3220**	**38**
Out		**3224**	**37**
Total		**6444**	**75**

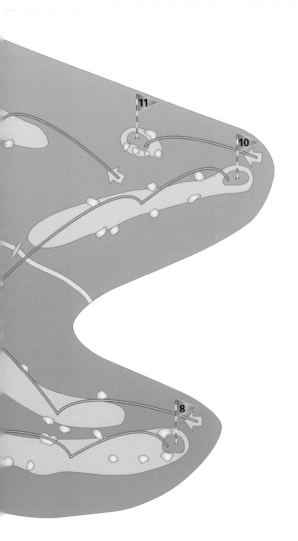

THE FIRST 12 OPEN CHAMPIONSHIPS were held at Prestwick, in Ayrshire, on the west coast of Scotland. It was the club itself that instigated the idea of a championship to determine the successor to Allan Robertson, who was generally accepted to be the finest player until his death in 1859.

Golf had been played over common land at Prestwick for many years and in 1851 a course of 12 holes was laid out. Major James Fairlie, a prominent figure in the formation of the club lured Tom Morris Snr from St. Andrews, and it was he who responsible for the original layout.

The first Open Championship was held on 17 October 1860 when eight professionals played three rounds of 12 holes in a single day. The winner with a total of 174 was Willie Park Sr of Musselburgh, his score being two less than that of Tom Morris Sr. Park won a further two championships at Prestwick, while Morris went on to complete four victories between 1861 and 1867.

A further six holes were added in 1883, but in 1925, when the club hosted its 24th Open, it was to be its last. Huge crowds swarmed over the course to follow Scots-born MacDonald Smith, who started the final round with a five-stroke lead. Amid the chaos, however, he completely collapsed and the title went to Jim Barnes. Partly because of this, and also because of its limited length and lack of space for parking and practice, it was felt that the course that had given birth to the idea of the championship 65 years before could no longer cope.

Prestwick continued to host the Amateur Championship until 1987, and to this day it retains many of its traditions and original features. Little has changed on the course for many years, and in the clubhouse can be seen a fine collection of golfing memorabilia linked to the original Open Championships.

ST ANDREWS

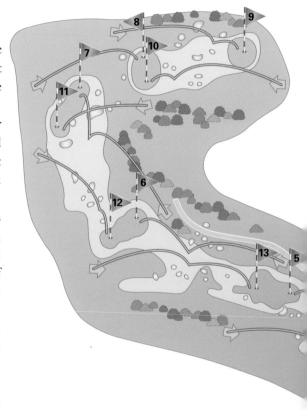

I N 1871 THE R&A JOINED UP with Prestwick and The Honourable Company of Edinburgh Golfers, then based at Musselburgh, and the next 22 championships were shared by the three clubs in rotation.

St Andrews hosted its first championship in 1873, played over two rounds of 18 holes, and the winner was Tom Kidd, a local man, with a score of 179. It is uncertain as to when golf began at St Andrews, but it is known that the Old Course has been in existence in some form since the early fifteenth century.

The course has changed little since Tom Kidd's victory. It is unique in that there are seven double greens – the 2nd and 16th, 3rd and 15th, 4th and 14th, 5th and 13th, 6th and 12th, 7th and 11th, 8th and 10th, each pair, oddly, adding up to 18! Some of them are enormous, as large as an acre, and unless the approach shot is accurate, three or even more putts are commonplace.

The course is littered with both tiny pot bunkers and huge deep ones such as the terrifying Hell Bunker on the 14th that has caught out many of the greatest names in the game including Jack Nicklaus, who in the 1995 championship took ten strokes for the hole, having taken four strokes to get out. Many bunkers are hidden from view, and with all these quirky characteristics it can take years to master the course if ever at all. The secret is to avoid these bunkers and score well around the relatively short holes of 'The Loop' – the 7th to the 11th. The course favours a player who draws rather than fades the ball.

It opens with arguably the widest fairway in golf, running parallel with the 18th, with the second shot requiring precise judgement as the Swilcan Burn runs across the front of the green.

At the far end of the course lies one of the toughest short holes in golf, the 11th, 'High Hole In', with the Eden estuary behind. With the green at a fierce angle sloping back to two of the deadliest bunkers, Hill and Strath, a three on this hole is always gratefully received.

The 17th, the Road Hole, is probably the most famous hole in golf. At this dog-leg right par four of 461 yards, with the Old

THE OLD COURSE, ST ANDREWS
(*as at 2000*)

Hole		Yards	Par
1	Burn	376	4
2	Dyke	413	4
3	Cartgate (out)	397	4
4	Ginger Beer	464	4
5	Hole O'Cross (out)	568	5
6	Heathery (out)	412	4
7	High (out)	388	4
8	Short	175	3
9	End	352	4
Out		3545	36

Hole		Yards	Par
10	Bobby Jones	379	4
11	High (home)	174	3
12	Heathery (home)	314	4
13	Hole O'Cross (home)	430	4
14	Long	581	5
15	Cartgate (home)	456	4
16	Corner of the Dyke	424	4
17	Road	455	4
18	Tom Morris	357	4
In		**3570**	**36**
Out		**3545**	**36**
Total		**7115**	**72**

Course Hotel on the right, every shot needs to be absolutely precise to have a chance of a par. To the right of the green lies a bank, a road (from which there is no relief) and then a wall leading to out of bounds. (Until the early 1960s a railway line ran along this part of the course from St Andrews out to Leuchars some four miles away.) To the left is the small, deep and steep Road Hole Bunker that cuts into the green so much that it is not uncommon for players to putt into it. It has ruined many a score, none more famous than that of Japan's Tommy Nakajima in the 1978 Open. Safely on the green in two, he putted into the bunker, took four shots to get out and a ten went down on his card when a four had looked likely minutes earlier.

In the 1984 championship a wayward second shot by Tom Watson finished beside the wall, ending his hopes of emulating Harry Vardon's six titles.

The 18th at St Andrews appears to be a straightforward par four of 354 yards, played back towards the town, but at the front of the green lies The Valley of Sin. A weak approach will run back into it, and then fine judgement is required to get down in two for a par. Some of the most dramatic finishes in the history of the championship have been seen around this green, none more so than those of 1970 (Jack Nicklaus and Doug Sanders) and 1995 (John Daly and Costantino Rocca).

St Andrews has hosted more Opens than any other course (26) and any Open held here has a special atmosphere of its own.

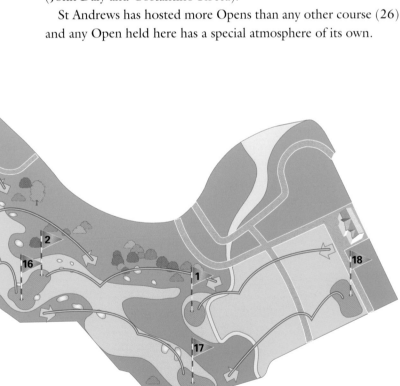

MUSSELBURGH

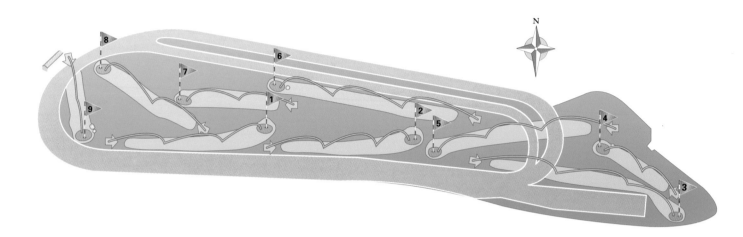

THE MUSSELBURGH LINKS lie a few miles to the east of Edinburgh and are arguably the oldest known. Originally a seven-hole course, it had an eighth added in 1832 and a ninth shortly afterwards. During the latter part of the nineteenth century as many as six golf clubs were based at Musselburgh and shared the links, the leading clubs being The Honourable Company, The Burgess Club, The Bruntsfield Club and The Royal Musselburgh Club.

Musselburgh was the scene of many of the great money matches, usually foursomes between the leading players of St Andrews and Musselburgh itself and in 1874 hosted its first Open Championship. The winner, with a then record score of 159 for two rounds of 18 holes was Mungo Park.

A further five Open Championships were played over the links until 1891 when The Honourable Company moved to Muirfield and took the championship with them. They felt that Musselburgh had become too crowded, and with the course surrounded by a racetrack that remains to this day, expansion of the course was impossible. When The Royal Musselburgh Club moved to a new course designed by James Braid at nearby Prestonpans, a rapid decline in the Musselburgh links followed.

A move to restore the links to their former glory has to some extent worked, but the course is now little more than a curiosity of the past. It is however a 'fun' nine holes to play and at the far end of the course the public house, 'Mrs Forman's', that has been in existence for well over a hundred years, can still be visited.

MUSSELBURGH (*as at 1889*)

Hole		Yards
1	The Graves	350
2	Linkfield	420
3	Mrs. Forman's	500
4	Sea Hole	190
5	The Table	360
6	The Bathing Coach	410
7	Hole Across	280
8	The Gas	320
9	Home Hole	170
Total		3000

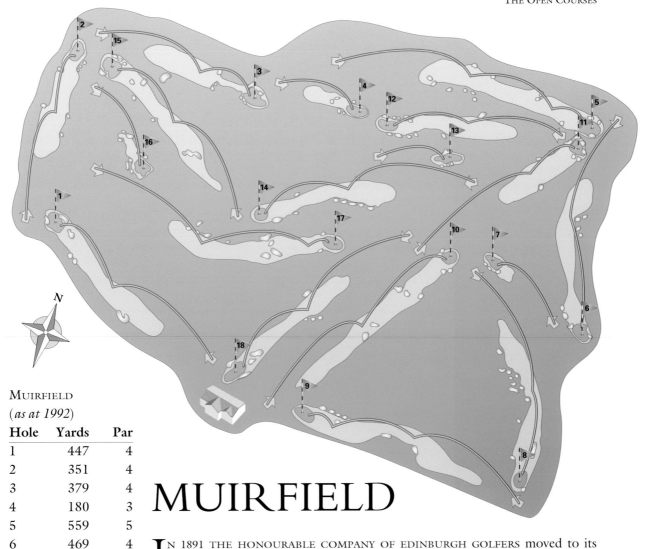

MUIRFIELD
(*as at 1992*)

Hole	Yards	Par
1	447	4
2	351	4
3	379	4
4	180	3
5	559	5
6	469	4
7	185	3
8	444	4
9	504	5
Out	**3518**	**36**
10	475	4
11	385	4
12	381	4
13	159	3
14	449	4
15	417	4
16	188	3
17	550	5
18	448	4
In	**3452**	**35**
Out	**3518**	**36**
Total	**6970**	**71**

MUIRFIELD

In 1891 THE HONOURABLE COMPANY OF EDINBURGH GOLFERS moved to its third home, Muirfield, at Gullane, some twenty miles east of Edinburgh, and has remained there ever since. Originally laid out by Old Tom Morris, the course came to the fore when updated by Harry Colt and then in the 1920s by Tom Simpson. Muirfield is regarded by many as the finest and fairest of courses on the Open rota, but also one of the toughest.

Like both Prestwick and St Andrews, Muirfield maintains many of the traditions of the game, but whereas the courses at St Andrews are public property, Muirfield is a very private club.

Unlike many links courses that run out for the first nine and back for the second, Muirfield is made up of two loops, the first clockwise and the second anti-clockwise. There are no trees and no water hazards but plenty of rough!

The first Open to be played at Muirfield was in 1892, and it was the first to be played over 72 holes. The winner was Harold Hilton, an amateur from Hoylake, and he remains one of only three amateurs to win the title. The club has regularly hosted the championship ever since, with some of the game's greatest players winning here – Vardon, Braid, Hagen, Cotton, Player, Nicklaus, Trevino, Watson and Faldo have all been successful.

ROYAL ST GEORGE'S, SANDWICH

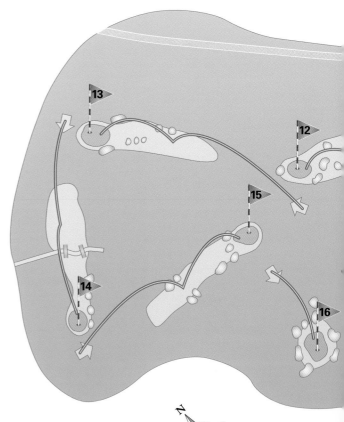

IN 1887 DR WILLIAM PURVES, a Scot based in London and a member at Royal Wimbledon, decided to set up a links course for him and his friends. The story has it that he and two friends surveyed the coastline from the church tower at Sandwich and on seeing the links declared them to be of perfect potential. The land belonged to the Earl of Guildford, who granted him a lease on 320 acres and The St George's Club was formed.

The course took shape with remarkable speed and in 1892 the club hosted the first Amateur Championship. Just two years later, following a visit from an R&A delegation to inspect the course, Sandwich hosted its first Open Championship, remarkably just seven years after its inception.

The championship went to J.H. Taylor and the club hosted a further eight until 1949. Again, like Muirfield it produced many great champions – Harry Vardon in 1899 and 1911 (after a play-off with Arnaud Massy), Walter Hagen twice (1922 and 1928), Henry Cotton in 1934 and Bobby Locke in 1949 following a play-off with Harry Bradshaw.

A gap of 32 years then followed, mainly because the tiny cobbled streets in the town made access difficult and Sandwich could not cope with the demands of a modern day-championship. But in 1981 the Open returned, following the building of a by-pass and modernizing of the course by the architect Frank Pennink. The club now remains firmly on the championship rota. Texan Bill Rogers putted his way to glory that year and famous victories by Sandy Lyle and Greg Norman have followed.

Royal St George's is often described as the Muirfield of the south and on a pleasant summer's day with the sun shining, the larks singing and with its luscious

ROYAL ST GEORGE'S, SANDWICH (*as at 1993*)

Hole	Yards	Par
1	441	4
2	376	4
3	210	3
4	468	4
5	421	4
6	155	3
7	530	5
8	418	4
9	389	4
Out	**3408**	**35**

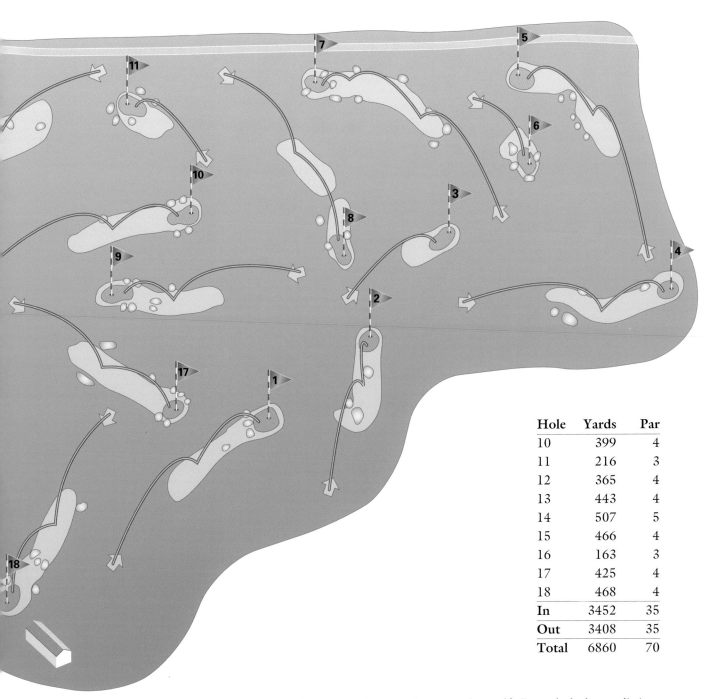

Hole	Yards	Par
10	399	4
11	216	3
12	365	4
13	443	4
14	507	5
15	466	4
16	163	3
17	425	4
18	468	4
In	3452	35
Out	3408	35
Total	6860	70

turf there are few more pleasant places to play golf. Every hole has a distinct character of its own, and the last six holes provide one of the toughest finishes to any links course.

The course has four superb short holes, the 155 yard 'Maiden' 6th requiring a perfectly judged tee shot to avoid a cluster of bunkers awaiting an errant shot. The par five 14th is another dangerous hole where the 'Suez Canal' to the right of the fairway lures many a tee shot. At 468 yards the 18th is surely one of the most exacting finishing holes in championship golf. Sandwich is without doubt a wonderful links test.

THE ROYAL LIVERPOOL GOLF CLUB, HOYLAKE

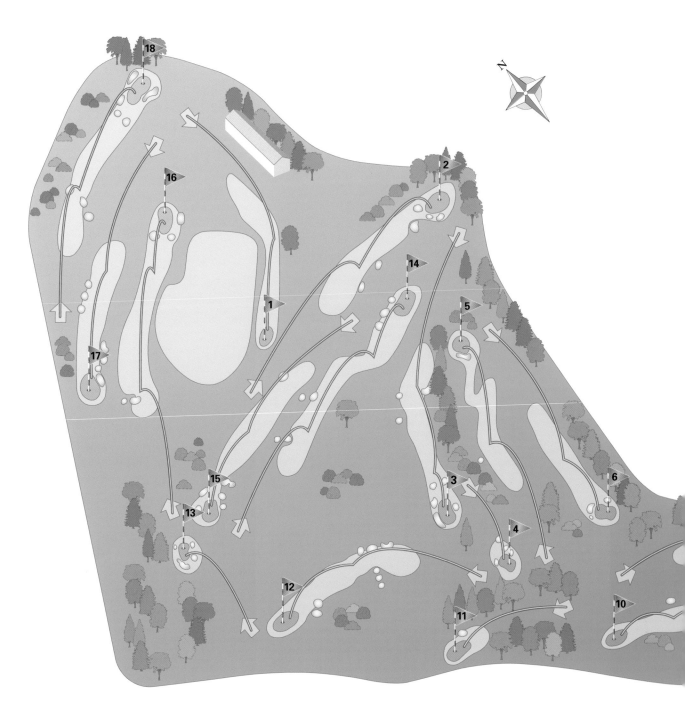

IN ENGLAND ONLY ROYAL BLACKHEATH AND ROYAL NORTH DEVON are older than Royal Liverpool, or Hoylake as it is better known. The club was founded in 1869 and has an enormous amount of history behind it. Set up by a group of exiled Scots, in the main businessmen working in Liverpool, the club was for some years run from The Royal Hotel adjacent to the course. It was not until 1895 that it moved to its present clubhouse.

The first Amateur Championship was hosted here in 1885, the first English Amateur in 1925, and it also held the first matches between England and Scotland, Britain and the United States and the Home Internationals.

Three players in particular were famous Hoylake members, of whom the most notable were Harold Hilton and John Ball, and the other was Jack Graham, who was four times a semi-finalist in the Amateur in the first decade of the twentieth century. Both Ball and Hilton won the Open as amateurs, Ball at Prestwick in 1890 and Hilton twice, at Muirfield in 1892 and at Hoylake in its first Open of 1897.

Hoylake is set on a sandy stretch of land on the shores of the River Dee, originally a rabbit warren and also used as a racecourse. The first nine holes were designed by George Morris, a nephew of Old Tom, and in 1871 a further nine were added.

The greatest requirement for a successful score at Hoylake is straightness, for there is an abundance of out of bounds. The first hole is one of the most terrifying opening holes in golf, with out of bounds all the way down the right hand side, and many other holes are the same, notably the 7th and 16th.

Hoylake has four par threes, two long and two short, and no championship course offers a better selection. Its finishing holes also offer a great challenge, notably in a wind, and to walk away from the final green having matched par on the final four holes is a fine achievement.

In all Hoylake has played host to ten Open Championships, and has seen many famous victories, such as Sandy Herd's win in 1902 using the new rubber-core Haskell ball. Frenchman Arnaud Massy won in 1907, Walter Hagen was successful in 1924 by a single stroke, and in 1930 Bobby Jones won here *en route* to completing the Grand Slam. In 1947 Irishman Fred Daly crossed the Irish Sea to take the title, and in 1956 Peter Thomson completed his hat-trick here, but none was more popular or emotionally charged than Roberto de Vicenzo's win in 1967, when he was finally successful having been competing in the event for twenty years.

It was decided after de Vicenzo's win that the club could no longer cope with the Open's ever-increasing demands in terms of parking and space for the Tented Village.

Hoylake remains a wonderful golf course, with a tradition of superb greens, and is also a most welcoming club. Inside the clubhouse itself a fine collection of golfing memorabilia can be seen, much of it relating to Hoylake's two amateur Open Champions, Harold Hilton and John Ball. There are few finer places to be found in Britain for one to spend a day golfing.

ROYAL LIVERPOOL,
HOYLAKE (*as at 1967*)

Hole	Yards	Par
1	421	4
2	426	4
3	491	5
4	196	3
5	450	4
6	389	4
7	193	3
8	492	5
9	393	4
Out	**3451**	**36**
10	404	4
11	201	3
12	460	4
13	158	3
14	515	5
15	459	4
16	529	5
17	418	4
18	400	4
In	**3544**	**36**
Out	**3451**	**36**
Total	**6995**	**72**

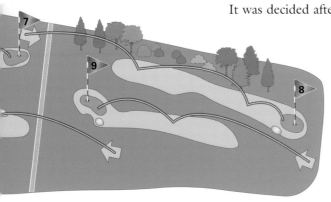

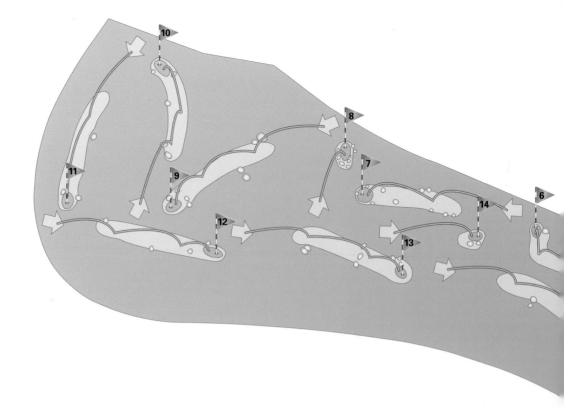

BETTER KNOWN SIMPLY AS DEAL, the Royal Cinque Ports Golf Club was founded in 1892 and hosted the first of its two Open Championships just 17 years later in 1909.

Running north to south at both the start and finish, with four holes at the far end near to Royal St George's at right angles to the general line of play, Deal is without doubt a great test of golf. With the prevailing wind coming from the south-west, it has the effect of not really helping going out as it comes over one's left shoulder, and it certainly does not help at all coming home. In fact, when played into a stiff wind the closing five or six holes offer as stern a test as is possible.

J.H. Taylor comfortably won the 1909 Open, by a margin of four strokes, and the club hosted the first championship to be held after the First World War, in 1920. Despite starting with two 80s George Duncan took the title, having been 13 strokes behind Abe Mitchell at the halfway stage.

The 1949 Championship was scheduled to be played at Deal, but an abnormally high tide caused extensive flooding and the championship reverted to Royal St George's, just a mile or so along the coast.

The club never had the chance to host the event again, as it was felt that the narrowness of the course and its lack of accessibility make it unsuitable for a modern-day championship.

Deal, like so many of the championship courses, is a wonderful place to play golf. It has hosted many of the top amateur events for both men and ladies and is the home of the Halford Hewitt Challenge Cup, a foursomes competition played for annually by the leading public school old boys teams.

Deal and nearby Royal St George's are best described in the words of the legendary Bernard Darwin:

ROYAL CINQUE PORTS, DEAL *(as at last Open of 1920)*

Hole	Yards	Bogey
1	330	4
2	376	4
3	476	5
4	150	3
5	475	5
6	282	4
7	383	4
8	136	3
9	454	4
Out	**3062**	**36**

ROYAL CINQUE PORTS GOLF CLUB, DEAL

Hole	Yards	Par
10	367	4
11	441	4
12	471	4
13	431	4
14	195	3
15	417	4
16	483	5
17	372	4
18	414	4
In	3591	36
Out	3062	36
Total	6653	72

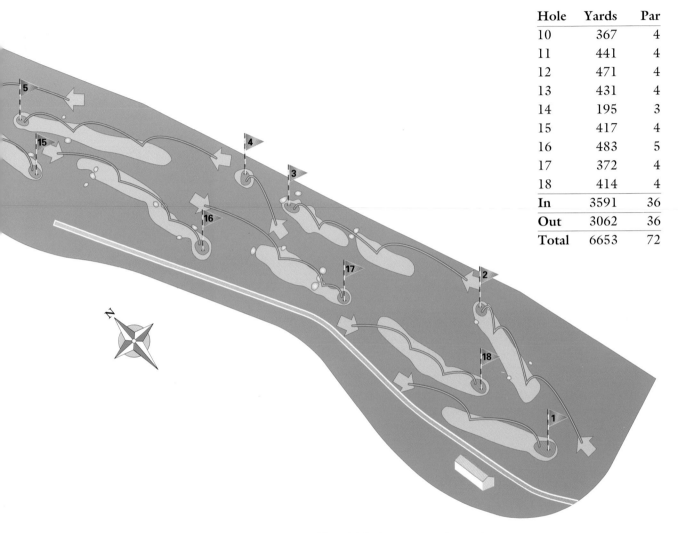

'Deal is a truly great course. I incline myself to think the most testing and severe of all the championship courses ... yet it is not in these stern and almost sombre conditions that I best like to think of Deal or Sandwich. My daydreams are rather of them on a day of sunshine and light breeze – it is perhaps because it chances that here are the first really great courses that I ever saw, that this smiling corner of the earth's surface has for me something that no other spot, not even perhaps St Andrews can quite equal. The larks seem to me to sing a little louder and more cheerfully there and the grass to have a more poignantly delicious taste of garlic. I am sure no other cliffs are so shining white as those beyond Pegwell Bay or that there is no shipping like that through the big plate-glass windows at Deal. Long may these things remain unchanged for golfing generations to enjoy.'

ROYAL TROON

In 1923 TROON (which became Royal Troon in 1978, its centenary year) was the eighth club to host the Open Championship.

Although it is believed that four or five holes may have existed as early as 1870 it was not until 1878 that the club was formed at the instigation of a local doctor, John Highet. The 6th Duke of Portland owned the prospective land and permission was granted to set up a course. Over many years the course has been altered slightly by many leading names in golf course architecture, notably Willie Fernie, the 1883 Open champion and Troon's club professional, James Braid, Dr Alister Mackenzie of Augusta fame and Frank Pennink.

Set on the Ayrshire coast with the Isle of Arran in sight across the Firth of Clyde, Troon is a truly marvellous course. The first nine holes run true south, with the back nine running north back to the clubhouse and more often than not played into the wind. Like so many of the great championship links courses, Troon has the severest of finishing holes and there are many famous holes spread over the links.

The clubhouse at Troon is a fine building with its windows almost touching the back of the 18th green, and the club owns many fine golfing antiques, none rarer than a set of eight clubs believed to date back to Stuart times.

The course boasts both the longest and shortest holes in Open Championship golf. At 577 yards the 6th is the longest, while the 8th, at just 126 yards, is the shortest. Originally named the 'Ailsa', the hole eventually

ROYAL TROON (*as at 1997*)

Hole		Yards	Par
1	Seal	364	4
2	Black Rock	391	4
3	Gyaws	379	4
4	Dunure	557	5
5	Greenan	210	3
6	Turnberry	577	5
7	Tel-e-Kebir	402	4
8	Postage Stamp	126	3
9	The Monk	423	4
Out		**3429**	**36**

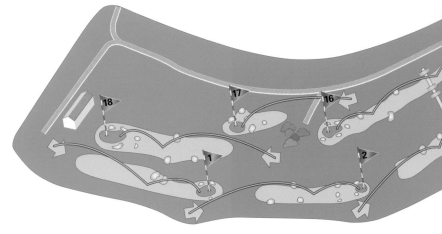

became known as the 'Postage Stamp' and has also been called 'golf's philatelic nightmare'! No doubt the German amateur Herman Tissies would have had stronger words for it after he had played it in the 1950 Open. Following 13 bunker shots he finally holed out in 15!

Turning for home the 11th provides a fearsome test. A long drive is required to make the carry, gorse and rough cut in close to the left of the fairway, and for good measure the Glasgow to Ayr railway line runs the entire length of the hole just to the right of the fairway! From here in there is no respite as every hole provides a challenge of its own.

The club has played host to every possible amateur event for both men and ladies and so far has hosted seven Open championships. Its first Open of 1923 was won by Englishman Arthur Havers, by a single shot from Walter Hagen. Twenty-seven years passed before the championship returned, in 1950, and Bobby Locke won his third title. In 1962 over-enthusiastic crowds caused chaos trying to follow Arnold Palmer to victory, and every championship since has provided drama and fine winners in Tom Weiskopf, Tom Watson, Mark Calcavecchia and Justin Leonard.

On a pleasant summer's day, with the beautiful Isle of Arran in view across the water, there are few better places to play the game, but when a good wind blows at Troon it is one of the toughest tests in golf.

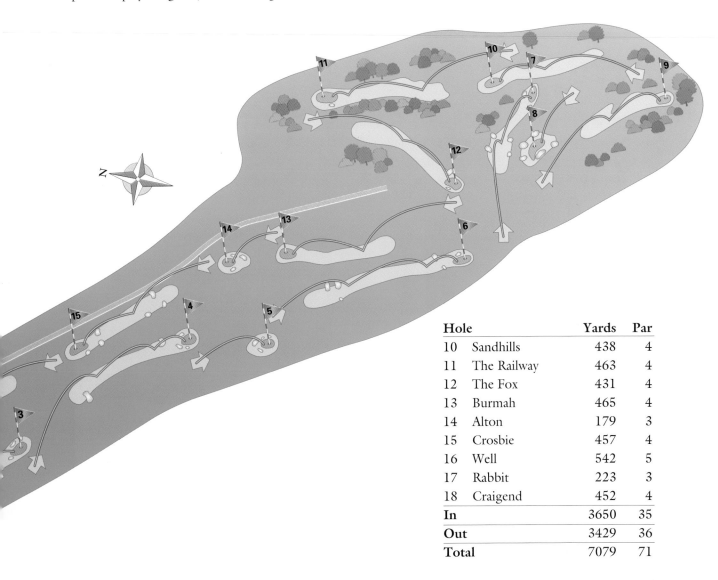

Hole		Yards	Par
10	Sandhills	438	4
11	The Railway	463	4
12	The Fox	431	4
13	Burmah	465	4
14	Alton	179	3
15	Crosbie	457	4
16	Well	542	5
17	Rabbit	223	3
18	Craigend	452	4
In		3650	35
Out		3429	36
Total		7079	71

ROYAL LYTHAM AND ST ANNES

T HE MOST NORTHERLY OF A SERIES of famous links courses on the Lancashire coast, Royal Lytham and St Annes is a magnificent course and a great challenge.

Originally set up in 1886, it moved to its current site in 1897. By 1903 it had a membership of more than 750, an enormous number at the time, and this helped to fund the building of a fine new clubhouse which is still in use today. An adjacent Dormy House was added in 1912 that has provided hospitality and warmth for thousands of weary golfers over the years.

Much of the original design of the course is credited to the then professional, George Lowe, who had moved from nearby Hoylake, but other leading architects such as Harry Colt and Herbert Fowler were involved, and more recently in the 1950s Ken Cotton made various alterations to modernize the course.

Lytham is unique as an Open Championship course for two reasons. First, it is the only one to start with a par three (although the 1st at Muirfield was a par three until the 1920s); secondly, it is surrounded by houses and the Preston to Blackpool railway line. Despite this, and the fact that it is half a mile or so from the sea, Lytham plays like a true links course and its greens are as fine as any. The first nine is where a score must be made, for the back nine, some 250 yards longer and invariably played into the wind, is a fearsome test.

Lytham played host to the Open Championship for the first time in 1926 (the year it was granted its Royal Charter) and one of the most famous strokes played in golfing history was made that very year. Paired with fellow American Al Watrous, the legendary amateur Bobby Jones left his tee shot on the 71st hole bunkered to the left of the hole, some 170 yards from the green. Tied at the time, they were the only two in with a chance of victory, and when Watrous put his second safely on the green the title seemed to be in his grasp. However, using his mashie Jones played the shot of a lifetime from a clean lie in the bunker and put his ball inside his opponent's. Visibly shaken, Watrous three-putted, Jones made his par four, and with a four to a five on the final hole victory was his by two strokes from a seemingly impossible position. A commemorative plaque can still be seen to this day at the spot from where he played the stroke.

Lytham was firmly on the map and has regularly hosted championships since, including the Ryder Cup and many other leading events. Many memorable Opens have been witnessed here, and there are great names on the role of honour. Bobby Locke was victorious in 1952 by a single stroke; the next two were won after play-offs by Peter Thomson and Bob Charles; and in 1969 Tony Jacklin restored British pride following a drought of 18 years without a 'home' win.

Gary Player was the only person under par in 1974 when he took the title after putting left-handed on the final hole with his ball lodged against the clubhouse wall, and in 1979 Severiano Ballesteros defied the odds by hitting his ball all over the course but still became champion. He returned to Lytham nine years later and with a scintillating display of golf beat Nick Price and Nick Faldo on a memorable last day. In 1996 Tom Lehman became the first American professional to win the title at Lytham with a wonderful display of scoring under perfect conditions.

Lytham is a truly great championship course and it is highly deserving of its Open status. Only in the kindest of weather conditions does it ever succumb to low scoring. More often than not there is enough wind to test the best players to their absolute limit, particularly over its closing holes. Many a round has been ruined at the long par four 17th, usually played into the wind and littered with bunkers.

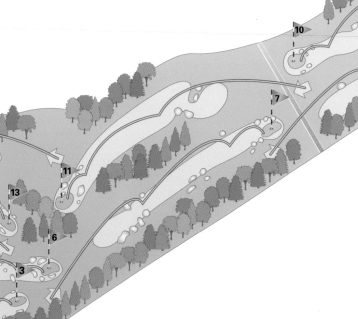

Royal Lytham

(*as at 1996*)

Hole	Yards	Par
1	206	3
2	437	4
3	457	4
4	393	4
5	212	3
6	490	5
7	553	5
8	418	4
9	164	3
Out	**3330**	**35**

Hole	Yards	Par
10	334	4
11	542	5
12	198	3
13	342	4
14	445	4
15	463	4
16	357	4
17	467	4
18	414	4
In	**3562**	**36**
Out	**3330**	**35**
Total	**6892**	**71**

CARNOUSTIE

Hole		Yards	Par
1	Cup	407	4
2	Gulley	462	4
3	Jockie's Burn	342	4
4	Hillocks	412	4
5	Brae	411	4
6	Long	578	5
7	Plantation	412	4
8	Short	183	3
9	Railway	474	4
Out		**3681**	**36**

CARNOUSTIE (*AS at 1999*)

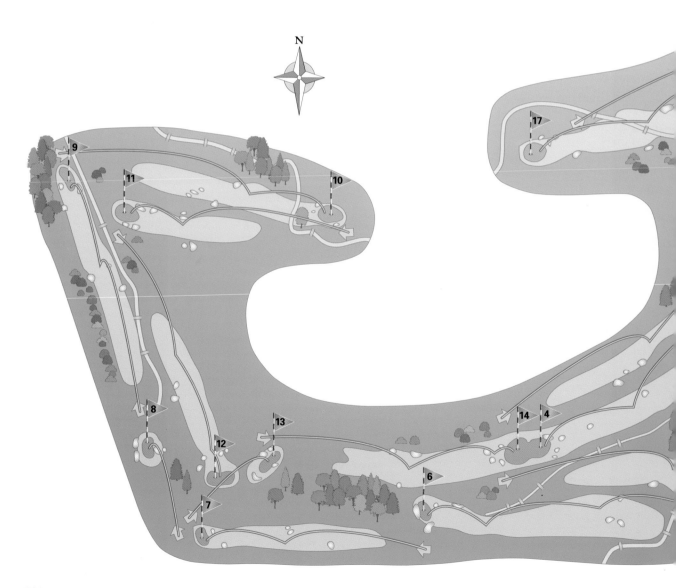

Hole		Yards	Par
10	South America	466	4
11	Dyke	383	4
12	Southward Ho	479	5
13	Whins	169	3
14	Spectacles	515	5
15	Lucky Slap	472	4
16	Barry Burn	250	3
17	Island	459	4
18	Home	487	4
In		**3680**	**36**
Out		**3681**	**36**
Total		**7361**	**72**

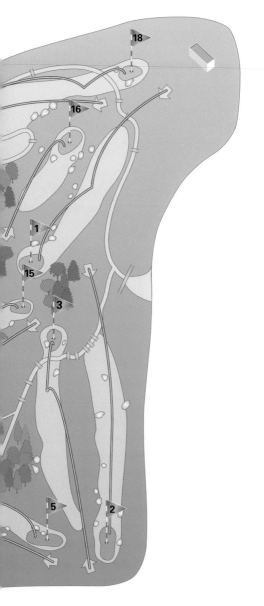

As with many of the famous old courses on the east coast of Scotland there is no certainty as to when golf was first played at Carnoustie, but parish records confirm that the game was played as early as 1560.

A course of ten holes was laid out in 1842 by the great Allan Robertson, extended to 18 by Old Tom Morris in 1867 and finally revamped in 1926 by James Braid. The main feature of the course is the Barry Burn, a winding stretch of water that either crosses or comes into play on at least nine holes, none more so than on the 17th and 18th holes, possibly the most fearsome finish in golf.

Lying on the north shore of the Tay Estuary, some 11 miles across the water from St Andrews, the town of Carnoustie is one of the true 'homes' of golf. Literally dozens of its sons have started life here and sought fame and golfing fortune around the globe, notably in the United States, the most famous being the Smith brothers, Alex, Willie and MacDonald, and also Stewart Maiden, who was Bobby Jones's coach.

Carnoustie's first Open Championship was held in 1931 when Tommy Armour, Edinburgh born but living in the States, won from Argentinian José Jurado. Six years later Henry Cotton played one of the great final rounds in Open history in appalling conditions to take the title against a field that included the entire American Ryder Cup team. Ben Hogan's victory of 1953 will be remembered as one of the finest, and in 1968 Gary Player took his second title, his three-wood second shot to the 14th 'Spectacles' hole securing victory over Jack Nicklaus and Bob Charles.

The year 1975 saw the beginning of Tom Watson's dominance of the championship for a decade, his triumph coming only after a play-off with Australian Jack Newton.

There followed a decline in the quality of the Carnoustie links, and it was a further 24 years before the championship returned, much credit for its eventual revival due to the Links Management Committee, its chairman the late Jock Calder and head greenkeeper John Philp.

Paul Lawrie's winning score of six over par in the 1999 championship reflects how severe a course it is. The links of Carnoustie do not have the beauty of other great championship courses but there are none tougher or more fearsome, particularly when the wind blows, which invariably it does!

It would appear that following its renaissance in 1999, Carnoustie is firmly back on the Open rota. Anyone who witnessed the final scenes of Frenchman Jean Van de Velde throwing away victory on the final hole is unlikely ever to see a more remarkable finish to a major golf event.

PRINCES

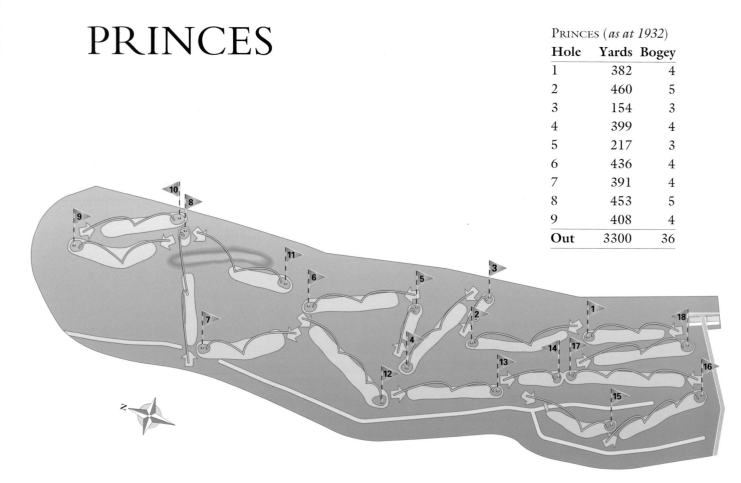

PRINCES (*as at 1932*)		
Hole	Yards	Bogey
1	382	4
2	460	5
3	154	3
4	399	4
5	217	3
6	436	4
7	391	4
8	453	5
9	408	4
Out	3300	36

THE PRINCES GOLF CLUB, adjacent to Royal St George's at Sandwich, and near to Deal, has hosted just one Open Championship, in 1932.

American Gene Sarazen was the winner by five strokes, having led after every round, and his four-round total of 283 was a record for the championship at the time. An eagle three on the 8th in the final round helped secure his success, as well as the advice he took from his trusted caddie 'Skip' Daniels, whom Hagen had 'loaned' him four years earlier at Royal St George's. Sarazen went on to win the US Open just two weeks later.

Of the three clubs Princes has had by far the most turbulent history, having been affected badly by both World Wars, flooding and financial problems.

The course was laid out in 1906 by Sir Harry Mallaby-Deeley and the then secretary of the club P.M. Lucas (father of Walker Cup player 'Laddie' Lucas), and its main feature is a range of dunes known as The Himalayas.

Princes is a fine test of golf but has been somewhat overshadowed in terms of championships by its illustrious neighbour, Royal St George's. However work is currently beng carried out with the intention of restoring the course to its former glories. If one finds oneself in this golfing Mecca of Kent, a round of golf at Princes should not be overlooked.

Hole	Yards	Par
10	386	4
11	408	4
12	456	5
13	411	4
14	202	3
15	335	4
16	416	4
17	516	5
18	460	5
In	3590	38
Out	3300	36
Total	6890	74

INDEX

A

Aaron, Tommy 106
Adams, Jimmy 61, 63
Allen, Michael 161
Alliss, Percy 53
Alliss, Peter 53, 88, 130
Anderson, Jamie 13
Anderson, 'Tip' 101
Aoki, Isao 132, 136, 139, 153
Armour, Tommy 52–3
Ayton, Laurie 85
Azinger, Paul 154, 159

B

Baker–Finch, Ian 163–4
Balding, Al 84, 106
Ball, John Jr 14
Ball, Tom 28
Ballesteros, Severiano 135–7, 147, 148–9, 156–7
Barnes, Brian 107, 118, 120
Barnes, Jim 42
Bean, Andy 139, 145
Beck, Chip 163, 165
Bollinger 110–12
Bonallack, Sir Michael 8, 89, 107
Bottomley, Steven 174–5
Boxall, Richard 163
Bradshaw, Harry 73–4
Braid, James 15, 17, 19, 24, 26, 28, 30
Brand, Gordon Jr 165
Brickman, Brigadier 8
Broadhurst, Paul 162, 176
Brooks, Mark 172, 174–5
Brown, Eric 81, 83, 85–6, 87
Brown, Ken 139
Bulla, Johnny 64–5, 68–9, 70
Bullock, Fred 89
Burton, Dick 63, 64–5
Busson, Jack 63, 64–5

C

Cabrera, Angel 183
Calcavecchia, Mark 158–60
Calder, Jock 183
Campbell, Michael 174–5
Carbonetti, Horatio 139
Carnoustie 5, 7, 52–3, 62, 80–1, 107–8, 126, 183, 208–9
Casper, Billy 107–8, 109, 116
Cerda, Antonio 76–7, 81, 82, 84
Chapman, Robert 163
Charles, Bob 98–9
Clampett, Bobby 142–3, 144
Clark, Clive 113
Clarke, Darren 178–9
Cole, Bobby 122, 126

Coles, Neil 113, 121
Coltart, Andrew 184
Compston, Archie 47
Coody, Charles 117
Cook, John 165–7, 174
Cotton, Henry 57, 58–9, 62, 72
Couples, Fred 149, 159, 160, 164, 178, 180
Cox, Bill 63
Crampton, Bruce 84
Crenshaw, Ben 135–7, 139, 141

D

Daly, Fred 70–1
Daly, John 174–5
Daniels, Skip 54
Darwin, Bernard 48, 33
Davis, Rodger 136, 154
de Vicenzo, Roberto 105–6
DeFoy, Craig 117
Demaret, Jimmy 82
Duncan, George 36
Durnian, Denis 144, 146

E

Els, Ernie 165, 169, 177

F

Faldo, Nick 147, 154–5, 161–2, 165–7
Fallon, Johnny 65, 83
Faulkner, Max 76–7
Faxon, Brad 172, 174
Fazio, George 80, 83
Feherty, David 159
Fernandez, Vincente 116–7, 141
Ferries, Jim 82
Floyd, Raymond 128, 134, 141, 144, 165
Forsbrand, Anders 172
Frost, David 154, 184–5
Eugol, Ed 83

G

Garaialde, Jean 98
Garcia, Sergio 171, 183
Gates, Martin 163
Ghezzi, Vic 70
Goalby, Bob 196
Grady, Wayne 158–60
Graham, David 141, 150–1
Green, Hubert 122, 128, 130
Green, Ken 154

H

Hagen, Walter 38, 40, 46–7, 48–9
Halberg, Gary 163
Hammond, Donnie 165

Harwood, Mike 163–4
Haskell ball 20–1
Havers, Arthur 39
Hayes, Mark 130, 153
Hedblom, Peter 177
Henning, Harold 94, 113–15
Herd, Sandy 20–1
Hilton, Harold 15
Hogan, Ben 80–1
Hole, Frank 130
Horne, Reg 71
Horton, Tommy 113, 128
Huggett, Brian 96, 102
Huish, David 126
Hunt, Bernard 93
Huston, John 180
Hutchison, Jock 37

I

Irwin, Hale 122, 136, 144–6

J

Jack, Reid 89
Jacklin, Tony 109–10
Jacobsen, Peter 148, 161–2
James, Mark 129, 136
Jantzen, Lee 180–1
Job, Nick 141
Jones, Bobby 43–4, 45, 50–1

K

Kidd, Tom 12
King, Sam 72, 73, 81, 82
Kirkwood, Joe 58
Kite, Tom 128, 132, 151
Kuramato, Masahiro 142

L

Lacey, Charles 62
Langer, Bernhard 140–1, 143, 144, 149, 150, 154, 168
Lawrie, Paul 183–5
Leadbetter, David 155
Lee, Trevino 116–17, 118–19
Lees, Arthur 71
Lehman, Tom 176–7
Lema, Tony 100–1
Leonard, Justin 178–9
Little, Lawson 64, 68
Littler, Gene 96
Locke, Bobby 67, 73–4, 75, 79, 85–6
Longmuir, Bill 136, 148
Lu, Liang-Huan 116-7
Luna, Santiago 163
Lyle, Sandy 150–1

M

MacKenzie, Keith 8
Mahaffey, John 126
Maltbie, Roger 130
Mangrum, Lloyd 80, 81, 83
Marsh, Graham 128–9, 144–5
Mason, Carl 139
Massy, Arnaud 27
McCormack, Mark 91
McCumber, Mark 177
McGinley, Paul 176–7
McNulty, Mark 145, 162
Medlin, 'Squeaky' 173
Mickleson, Phil 181
Miguel, Sebastian 102
Miller, Johnny 128–9
Mitchell, Abe 36
Mize, Larry 154, 172
Morgan, Dr Gill 139
Morris, Tom Jr 11–12
Morris, Tom Sr 11–12
Mudd, Jodie 164
Muirfield 15, 19, 26, 32, 48–9, 60, 72, 89, 104, 118–19, 138–9, 154–5, 165–7, 197
Musselburgh 13, 14, 196

N

Nagle, Kel 92–3
Nakajima, Tommy 132, 153
Nelson, Byron 62, 83
Nelson, Larry 144
Newton, Jack 126–7, 128, 139
Nicklaus, Jack 104, 113–15, 132–4
Norman, Greg 147, 152–3, 168–9

O

O'Connor, Christy Jr 150
O'Connor, Christy Sr 87, 95, 101, 134
O'Meara, Mark 180–2
Olazabal, José-Maria 150, 159, 165, 167
Oldcorn, Andrew 163
Oosterhuis, Peter 113, 126, 132–5, 142, 3
Open Championship: 10–187
Open courses 192–213
Open milestones 188–90
Open records 191
Open results 214–18
Open statistics 219–20
Osaki, Norio 132
Owen, Simon 132–4

P

Padgham, Alf 61
Palmer, Arnold 91, 94–5, 96
Pampling, Rodney 183
Park, Mungo 13
Park, Willie Jr 14
Park, Willie Sr 11
Parnevik, Jesper, 172–3, 178, 9, 181–2
Parry, Craig 162, 184–5
Pate, Jerry 128, 139

Pate, Steve 165–6
Pavin, Corey 168, 174
Perry, Alf 60
Philip, John 183
Pickworth, Ossie 81
Platts, Lionel 102
Player, Gary 7, 89, 107–8, 122–3
Pose, Martin 161
Prestwick 11–14, 22, 28, 34, 39, 42, 192–3
Price, Nick 172–3
Princes 210
Pyman, Ian 169

R

Ray, Ted 32
Rees, Dai 60, 68–9, 81, 82, 94–5
Reid, Jack 89
Rivero, José 150
Roberts, Loren 180
Robertson, Allan 11
Robson, Fred 42
Rocca, Costantino 174–5
Rodgers, Phil 96, 98–9, 104
Rogers, Bill 140–1
Rose, Justin 181–2
Ross, MacKenzie 130
Royal Birkdale 82, 94–5, 102, 116–17, 128–9, 144–5, 163–4, 180–2, 212
Royal Cinque Ports Golf Club 29, 36, 202–3
Royal Liverpool Golf Club 15, 20–1, 27, 33, 40, 50–1, 61, 70–1, 84, 105–6, 200–1, 206–7
Royal Lytham and St Annes 43–4, 79, 87–8, 98–9, 109–10, 122–3, 135–7, 156–7, 176–7
Royal Portrush 76–7, 211
Royal St George's 18, 23, 31, 38, 46–7, 58–9, 63, 73–4, 140–1, 150–1, 168–9, 198–9
Royal Troon 75, 96, 120–1, 142–3, 204–5, 158–60, 178–9
Ruiz, Leopoldo 88
Russell, Raymond 182

S

Sanders, Doug 113–15
Sarazen, Gene 54
Scott, Syd 82, 89
Senior, Peter 163, 168
Shankland, Bill 65, 109
Sherry, Gordon 174
Shute, Denny 55
Sjoland, Patrick 183
Smith, Dick 85
Smith, MacDonald 42
Smyth, Des 142
Snead, Sam 68–9
Souchak, Mike 84
Spence, Bill 82
Spence, Jamie 162
St Andrews 12–13, 17–18, 24, 30, 37,

45, 55, 64–5, 68–9, 83, 85–6, 92–3, 100–1, 194–5, 113–15, 132–4, 148–9, 161–2, 174–5
Stadler, Craig 140, 144, 154–5
Stephens, Wayne 158–9
Stewart, Payne 150, 159–60
Stranahan, Frank 70–1, 76, 81, 84, 177
Sunnesson, Fanny 166
Sutton, Hal 144
Sutton, Norman 76
Suzuki, Norio 128

T

Tapping, David 178
Taylor, Gerard 154
Taylor, J.H. 15, 17, 18, 29, 33
Thomas, David 86–7, 88, 104
Thomson, Peter 82, 83, 84, 87–8, 102
Tissies, Herman 75
Tomori, Katsuyoshi 174–5
Torrance, Sam 161
Tupling, Peter 118
Turnberry 130–1, 152–3, 213, 272–3

V

Van de Velde, Jean 183–5
van Donck, Flory 84, 88, 89
Vardon, Harry 15, 17, 22, 31, 34
Vardon, Tom 22, 69
von Nida, Norman 68, 71, 72

W

Wadkins, Lanny 149
Ward, Charlie 71, 72, 73
Watson, Denis 144
Watson, Tom 125, 126–7, 130–1, 138–9, 142–3, 144–5
Watts, Brian 181–2
Weetman, Harry 76, 101
Weiskopf, Tom 120–1
Whitcombe, Charles 42, 60, 62
Whitcombe, Reg 42, 62, 63
White, Jack 23
Wolstenholme, Guy 89
Woods, Tiger 171, 177, 178–9, 180, 183–5
Woods, Walter 183
Woosnam, Ian 150, 152–3

Y

Yancey, Bert 120

Z

Zoeller, Fuzzy 142, 145, 168, 172